CAMBRIDGE LIBRARY COLLECTION

Books of enduring scholarly value

British and Irish History, Seventeenth and Eighteenth Centuries

The books in this series focus on the British Isles in the early modern period, as interpreted by eighteenth- and nineteenth-century historians, and show the shift to 'scientific' historiography. Several of them are devoted exclusively to the history of Ireland, while others cover topics including economic history, foreign and colonial policy, agriculture and the industrial revolution. There are also works in political thought and social theory, which address subjects such as human rights, the role of women, and criminal justice.

An Earnest Appeal for Mercy to the Children of the Poor

In eighteenth-century London, abandoned children were one of the social groups most affected by the harsh living conditions. Several charitable initiatives had endeavoured to alleviate the problem, not least the Foundling Hospital, of which Jonas Hanway (*c.*1712–86) was a governor. His tireless philanthropy and campaigning resulted in the 1762 Registers Bill, which required parishes to keep records of the poor children they looked after. In this tract, first published in 1766, Hanway uses information collected from these registers to demonstrate the appalling mortality rates of orphans in care in London, calling for radical reform. This work was instrumental in the passage of the 1767 act that resulted in a dramatic fall in the number of infant deaths over the following decade. It is a powerful exposé of the failures of the capital's care system, as well as a testament to the influence of philanthropic activism.

T0370763

Cambridge University Press has long been a pioneer in the reissuing of out-of-print titles from its own backlist, producing digital reprints of books that are still sought after by scholars and students but could not be reprinted economically using traditional technology. The Cambridge Library Collection extends this activity to a wider range of books which are still of importance to researchers and professionals, either for the source material they contain, or as landmarks in the history of their academic discipline.

Drawing from the world-renowned collections in the Cambridge University Library and other partner libraries, and guided by the advice of experts in each subject area, Cambridge University Press is using state-of-the-art scanning machines in its own Printing House to capture the content of each book selected for inclusion. The files are processed to give a consistently clear, crisp image, and the books finished to the high quality standard for which the Press is recognised around the world. The latest print-on-demand technology ensures that the books will remain available indefinitely, and that orders for single or multiple copies can quickly be supplied.

The Cambridge Library Collection brings back to life books of enduring scholarly value (including out-of-copyright works originally issued by other publishers) across a wide range of disciplines in the humanities and social sciences and in science and technology.

An Earnest Appeal for Mercy to the Children of the Poor

*Particularly Those Belonging to the Parishes
Within the Bills of Mortality*

Jonas Hanway

CAMBRIDGE
UNIVERSITY PRESS

CAMBRIDGE UNIVERSITY PRESS

Cambridge, New York, Melbourne, Madrid, Cape Town,
Singapore, São Paolo, Delhi, Mexico City

Published in the United States of America by Cambridge University Press, New York

www.cambridge.org
Information on this title: www.cambridge.org/9781108060929

This edition first published 1766
This digitally printed version 2013

ISBN 978-1-108-06092-9 Paperback

AN
EARNEST APPEAL
FOR
MERCY
To the CHILDREN of the POOR,

*particularly those belonging to the Parishes within the Bills of Mortality,
appointed by an Act of Parliament to be registered,*

BEING

*A general reference to the deserving conduct of some Parish Officers, and the
pernicious effects of the ignorance and ill judged parsimony of others.*

WITH SOME

COMPARATIVE VIEWS

of those Parishes and the Foundling Hospital;

*And Reasons for the necessity of such an hospital in these cities, to be maintained
for certain purposes only, and under certain restrictions.*

ALSO

*A Proposal for the more effectual preserving the Parish Children here, and
in other great cities and manufacturing towns, and rendering the
children of the poor in general pious, useful, and good subjects.*

By *Jonas Hanway, Esq;*

LONDON:

Sold by J. DODSLEY, in Pall-Mall; J. RIVINGTON, in St. Paul's Church-yard;
H. WOODFALL, at Charing-Cross, and N. YOUNG, under the Royal Exchange.
MDCCLXVI.
[Price Two Shillings.]

T O

ROSE FULLER, Efq;

DEAR SIR,

WHEN you engaged in the caufe of the infant poor (*a*), you intimated to me that *I muft fee to the execution of the defign.* I fhould indeed think myfelf happy to follow your example, and relieve the diftreffed fo far as my power extends; and I apprehend the *act* of the legiflature might be a means of fupplying the want of the Foundling Hofpital, as to the *good* part of that inftitution, without adminiftering to any of the evils it created.

With regard to the keeping a regifter of the infant poor within the bills of mortality, though the ignorance or inadvertency of fome parifh officers fhould not always admit of its being done with accuracy, it afforded the pleafing hopes that much the greater part of thofe officers might in a fhort time be brought into order, and reftore the reign of humanity.——The common people

(*a*) In 1762.

A 2

have

have underftood the tendency of the defign fo well that *they* call it *an act for keeping children alive.*

In all cures of the body, *politic* or *natural*, it is one great point gained to difcover the true nature of the difeafe, and the caufe whence it arifes. Many of our complaints are made from rumor, and many more from fafhion. Difficulties increafe in proportion as cuftom prevails over reafon; and whilft *Truth* is dif-guifed by *Prejudice*, it becomes an arduous tafk to find her out.

The regifter feems to point at the object we have been feeking for thefe thirty years, but more particu-larly in 1756, when parliament opened the Foundling Hofpital for an indifcriminate reception of infants. If we at length make fuch clear and ample difcoveries as may render that hofpital inftrumental to the relief of the friendlefs, on this fpot, without encouraging any tyranny in parochial officers, or any neglect of mater-nal tendernefs, the work will be accomplifhed.

As to cafes wherein the mother is living and in health, if fhe is relieved properly, and as the fpirit of our laws directs, the child at her breaft will be relieved alfo, in moft cafes, beyond all the art and contrivance of the acuteft politician.

I have

I have hitherto contented myfelf to animadvert on the act in general (*a*), waiting to fee the correction of faults which I could not control; and to praife where I could do it with truth and candor. I was determined to wait for a radical inveftigation of my fubject, before I carried my defign into full execution.

You will have the pleafure to fee that many happy effects already attend the regifter; tho' it is alfo as true that parochial officers, in feveral parifhes, are yet negligent, even to a crime, which in fome countries might be deemed capital.

One of our moft important inquietudes, efpecially in time of war, is that we want people, and yet many lives are loft by the groffeft negligence in our *police*. Is there any danger of our having too many *good people,* either in peace or war?

Fortunately for this nation the *poors rates,* fo frequently complained of, are the inftruments of preferving a vaft number of fubjects, particularly children, who are fo much more valuable than the aged.

If humanity, or religion, or the true love of our country, operate on the minds of men of fenfe in authority,

(*a*) Serious Confiderations on the falutary Defign of the Act of Parliament for a regular uniform Regifter of the Parifh Poor, 1762, fold by J. Rivington.

authority, no part of our poors rates will be mifapplied with regard to *infant life*, more than towards *adults*; or within the *bills of mortality*, more than in *any other part of the kingdom.*

I am well perfuaded, when fome of thefe fheets are perufed, the fame patriotic zeal which infpired you, and our compaffionate and difcerning friends, who adopted the falutary principles on which the *regifter* is founded, will induce them alfo to defend the act, and prevent its violation. And fo long as I am able, I will take my fhare in the glorious labors of humanity and public love! I am, with the higheft efteem,

DEAR SIR,

Your moft obedient,

humble Servant,

Red-Lion-Square,
May 10, 1766.

JONAS HANWAY.

CONTENTS.

SECT.

SECTION I.

Observations on the State of the Infant Parish Poor.

1. IT is generally acknowledged, that a *ninth part* of the whole people of *England* are congregated within the bills of mortality; and there is too great caufe to believe, that *a yet larger proportion of the iniquity of the whole land* is included in this fpace.

2. The *difeafe* which the *Foundling Hofpital* was intended to remedy was of fuch a nature, that *private* donations, in the meridian reputation of this inftitution, could by no means be adequate to the *cure*; fo that what was done previous to the adoption of the hofpital by the *public* in 1756, was fo fmall an object, in the great view of things, as to become of very little value, not only from the trifling number relieved, but from the manner of chufing them; and yet if the children moft in danger of death had been taken in, it might not have anfwered the end of acquiring any reputation, as a much fmaller number would have been preferved

3. Thefe *great cities* ought to be confidered in a very different light from all other parts of the kingdom : they are, with refpect to the reft, what the *head* is to the *limbs*; the calamities which befall them, by the greater mortality of inhabitants, neceffarily affecting the *whole*. If the *fame proportion* of mortality prevailed univerfally, the very exiftence of the nation muft ceafe.

The

4. The *poor's rates* are of very ancient ftanding, and might, by the true application, have anfwered all the ends in view; but whether a fuperftitious reverence for *cuftom*, a fear of trefpaffing on the office of overfeers and churchwardens, or that fo many infants annually were doomed to be offered up, is hard to fay. The evil remained long after it was difcovered, and exifts in a great degree, to this day.

5. If our *grandeur* and *opulence*, as a nation, are wounded in a vital part by the mortality of the poorer inhabitants of the *metropolis*, it muft neceffarily create fo much the greater drain from the *country* whence the general fupply arifes, and affect the *public expence* of lives. And as the productions of the earth ftand firft in rank, if we have not the firft view to the keeping a fufficient number of hands employed in agriculture, the whole will languifh and decay.

6. The idea of a Foundling Hofpital is built on the fuppofition of its being a *fecure* method of preferving lives; and our warmeft advocates for it reafoned on this principle: but this is taking for granted what experience contradicts. The method which nature has appointed is fo much fafer, as the experience of all countries proves, that it is only an urgent neceffity where parifh-rates for the poor are unknown, as in lands of popery, that drives them into this expedient.

7. We were not warranted to tax the whole for the local benefit of a part, which naturally fuperinduced an indifcriminate reception, though at the fame time it implied, that a child might be brought 3 or 400 miles at the almoft certain lofs of its life, unlefs the mother came with it, and then the expence would have been much better employed in keeping it at

home

home, even if an hofpital could have commanded any number of the beft nurfes, which was impoffible to be done. The event proved, that upon this plan, what was intended as a remedy became a difeafe; and a deftruction of lives was created, in feveral inftances, where it was meant to preferve them.

8. As the cafe now ftands, I fee no probability of extending the Foundling Hofpital fo far as to reach the difeafe we complain of, but by the *parifh-rates* in thofe parifhes which do not preferve their infant poor.—And if this is not done, I believe that a confiderable portion of the infants of the poor, born in thefe cities, will be loft.—Either the lawlefs commerce of the fexes, the poverty occafioned by vice, the indolence, ficknefs, or want of work, which in the courfe of human life will happen among fo vaft a multitude as 7 or 800,000 inhabitants, will alfo create peculiar evils which muft be provided for; and it proves but little, that the method of doing this is obvious, if the defect in the execution is equally apparent.

9. What is faid by the late ingenious and humane Dr. Hales of fpirituous liquors, may be applied to the conduct of fome parifh officers within the bills of mortality: he fays, " Of all the " miferies and plagues incident to human life, none are more " effectually deftructive than this, not even thofe three fore " judgments of *war, peftilence,* and *famine,* which after having " raged for fome time ceafe. But this *evil fpirit* is an unre- " lenting mercilefs enemy, that threatens deftruction from ge- " neration to generation."

The Doctor adds the following note, " The terrible deftruc- " tion of human lives appears from the following accounts:

In

In the year 1680, the chriſtenings, within the bills of
   mortality, were no more than   —   —   12747
From which number in 1700 they aroſe to   —   14639
And more remarkably in the year 1712 (notwithſtand-
   ing Queen Anne's *long war)* they were advanced to   15660
From that time they continually increaſed till the year
   1724, when they amounted to no leſs than   —   19370
But from that year to this (1750) they have decreaſed to 14320

So that the year 1750 produced *fewer* chriſtenings than the
year 1700.

The children likewiſe that *are born,* come into the world with
ſuch *bad conſtitutions,* that being ſickly and feeble, they die in
prodigious numbers under *five* years old. And many children,
inſtead of being nouriſhed by wholſome food, are ſoon con-
ſumed by the inflammatory ſpirits which muſt neceſſarily deſtroy a fabric ſo very ſlight and tender."

10. The ſame may be ſaid of *pariſh workhouſes,* ſo far as the
evil goes. To draw a parallel, one may with great truth aſſert,
that many children born of poor *idle* or *unfortunate* parents, tho'
they ſhould have the beſt conſtitutions, yet die in great numbers
under 5 years old; for tho' the humanity of the legiſlature has
been extended to them by a particular act of parliament, requiring a regiſter and authentic account, how the officers proceed
with them, yet ſome of theſe officers regard little more than
the *form,* and *this* very imperfectly. Many children inſtead
of being nouriſhed with care, by the foſtering hand or breaſt of
a wholſome country nurſe, are thruſt into the impure air of a
workhouſe, into the hands of ſome careleſs, worthleſs young
female, or decrepid old woman, and inevitably loſt for want of

ſuch

fuch means as the God of nature, *their* father as well as *ours*, has appointed for *their* prefervation

11. It is hard to fay, how many lives thefe cities have loft, or how many they yet lofe annually, by the poverty, filth, and vice of parents, which no public inftitutions in this land of free-dom can fave; and tho' we live on as fine a fpot as any the three kingdoms can boaft of, yet by being clofely built, and many living in confined places, and many too much congregated, joined to the fulphureous air created by fo vaft a number of coal fires, we muft not be furprized, that fo great a proportion as 20232 in 43101, or near 47 per cent. die under 2 years of age : this appears by an account now before me of 1756, 1757, and 1758. At thefe times the Foundling Hofpital was open for an indifcriminate reception; confequently the mortality there not being comprehended in the bills of mortality, rendered thofe bills fo much the lighter.

12. The calamities of human life, and the cuftoms of mankind, keep a pretty equal pace, and accordingly we find, that

There were chriftened in 1764	16374
Died under 2 years of age	8073
Which is $49\frac{1}{4}$ per cent.	
Remains	8301
Died more between 2 and 5 years old	1875

Which on 16374, is $11\frac{1}{4}$ per cent. and on 8301 is $22\frac{1}{2}$ per cent.

Such is the mortality within the bills of mortality; but this is happily no rule to judge of any other part of thefe kingdoms.

2

In the fame year 1764, were buried in all   —   23230
Which are more than the chriftenings, by   —   6856
And more than the ufual computation of lofs, by   1000

	Chriftenings	Burials	Decreafe
In 1756 we find —	14839	20872	6033
1757 — —		14053	21313	7260
1758 — —	14209	17576	* 3367

Which upon a medium is   —   —   5553

This happened during the Foundling Hofpital being open, and during the abfence of great numbers of people in war. Some years are peculiarly healthy, and in fome the fmall-pox fweeps off greater numbers, fo that a confiderable part of the great diminution of the decreafe in 1758, may be owing to the laft caufe, viz.

In 1756 died of the fmall-pox   —   —   1608
    1757 —   —   —   — 3296
    1758 —   —   —   — * 1273
    1765 —   —   —   — 2498

I do not mean to purfue the clue of the general mortality any further: the greater it is, the more we ftand in need of vigilance to preferve that part of the inhabitants, who are moft friendlefs and forfaken.

13. With regard to the *parifh infant poor*, it can hardly be ex-pected, that the beft regulated parifhes will preferve a greater proportion than 47 per cent. which is the general account. But the poor, who are our prefent object, exhibit a much more melancholy proportion.

Let

14. Let us do juſtice where we can, and particularly to *pariſh officers* who do their duty; and take the power out of the hands of thoſe who neglect it, by the utmoſt exertion of legal authority. Let the ſubject be ever ſo poor, humanity and religion do not therefore change their nature; the legiſlative authority remains the ſame; and we ought no more to ſuffer a child to die for want of the *common neceſſaries* of life, tho' he is born to labor, than one who is the heir to a dukedom. The extinction of thoſe who labor, would be more fatal to the community than if the number of the higheſt ranks of the people were reduced.

15. Thoſe who are idle, and not employed in ſomething good, are a *burthen*; and thoſe who are wicked, a *bane* to ſociety, whatever their condition be: and the more irreligious the more ungovernable.—In the mean time it ſeems as if the richer we grow, be our riches *real* or a great part *imaginary,* the more profligate the poor become; and that where luxury and expence moſt abound, there the poor ſooneſt loſe that ſimplicity of manners and fear of God, which the rich ſeem to be but ill inclined to teach, unleſs *they* are under circumſtances of *affliction.*

With regard to the ſobriety of the poor, the preſervation of life, and the preſervation of morals, go hand in hand: their *wickedneſs* is often the cauſe of their *mortality.*

16. Amidſt our various follies and iniquities, we ſtill aſpire at the characteriſtic of humane; tho' it is evident, in certain inſtances, there is not a nation upon earth, which acts more ſavagely than ourſelves. Thoſe who can bellow out for liberty and property, and raiſe a tumult in a *good* cauſe, or a *bad* one, will be *heard*; but what can the infant do? the child not arrived to his reaſon, who hath no parent, or none but ſuch as are

very

very poor, friendlefs or wicked; if the arm of humanity is not extended for the fupport of fuch in their infant ftate, they muft find a cruel grave, almoft as foon as they have feen the light.

17. As far as I can trace out the evil, there has been fuch devaftation within the bills of mortality, for half a century paft, that at a moderate computation 1000 or 1200 children have annually perifhed, under the direction of parifh officers. I fay under their direction, not that they ordered them to be *killed*; but that they *did not order* fuch means to be ufed, as are neceffary to keep them *alive*. How will this ftand recorded in our annals!

18. Never fhall I forget the evidence given at Guild-Hall, upon occafion of a mafter of a workhoufe of a large parifh, who was challenged for forcing a child from the breaft of the mother, and fending it to the Foundling Hofpital. He alledged this in his defence, " We fend all our children to the Foundling " Hofpital; we have not faved one alive for *fourteen years*. We " have no place fit to preferve them in; the air is too con- " fined."

When I witneffed to the appearance of the woman at the hofpital, and reported that the child was dead, of which the mother had not been acquainted, fhe fhrieked, and fell down as dead, exhibiting to the court a fcene of maternal tendernefs, which at once fhocked and delighted the fpectators.

It is to be obferved that the hofpital had not then been open much above *two* years of the *fourteen*, and notwithftanding the large fums then raifed on the poor's rates, no provifion was made by parifhes for fending a fingle infant into the country to be nurfed.

Of

[9]

19. Of the same nature was another parish, some years before the Foundling Hospital was opened, wherein it appeared, that of 54 children born, and taken into their workhouse, not one out-lived the year in which it was born or taken in. This seemed to be so incredible, that I went to the workhouse to enquire into the fact, and found it true. The workhouse was airy and well situated ; but *such was their nursing !*

The opening the hospital for an indiscrimate reception, afforded great relief to many such poor infants, but unhappily, as is well known, so many others were brought from the country, which ought not to have been brought, a great havoc of life was made, where there was very little or no mischief done before. Children were brought from places where they died at 13 and 14 in 100, under two years of age, to die at the rate of 60 or 70.

20. Tho' it may be difficult to extend our policy or humanity to every individual in distress, even within the bills of mortality, yet when we come to a whole parish, and see a public register appointed by *legislative* authority, wherein it appears that *parochial* authority hath superseded the *legislative*, by a gross neglect of the spirit of the *law*, insomuch that many infants have died under circumstances, but a small remove from *violence*; if we do not nicely inspect into such a calamity, how can we ask of heaven, that *mercy* of which we stand in so much need ourselves ?

This is the light in which I see the subject before us, and I hope that when others examine into it, such measures will be pursued, be it only for *five* or *six* parishes, or an *hundred*, as the exigency of the case shall require, upon the truest principles of policy and humanity.

C   S E C T.

S E C T. II.

Heads of the Act for the keeping regular, uniform, and annual Registers, of all Parish Poor Infants under a certain Age, within the Bills of Mortality.

THIS act begins with a plain, simple preamble. To have recited all that had past, would have required a volume, or made as doleful a tale, as *Hosier's injured ghost*. It says only, " Whereas the keeping regular, uniform, and annual registers of all parish poor infants under four years of age, within the bills of mortality, may be a means of preserving the lives of such infants.

1. That the churchwardens and overseers of the poor of every parish within the bills of mortality, or some one or more of them, shall, on or before the first day of July, in the present year 1762, provide, or cause to be provided, at the expence of their respective parish, one book of royal paper; and the book belonging to such respective parish wherein there *is* or *shall be* any *workhouse, hospital,* or other *house or place provided for the maintenance of the poor,* shall in every page be ruled with distinct columns, and the title of each column shall be wrote or printed in such page, agreeable to the schedule hereunto annexed, marked (A).

2. And the book belonging to each respective parish wherein there is not, nor shall be, any such workhouse, hospital house, or place, shall in every page be ruled with distinct columns, and

5   the

the title of each column fhall be wrote or printed in fuch page, agreeable to the fchedule hereunto annexed, marked (B).

3. That the faid churchwardens and overfeers of the poor, or fome one or more of them, fhall enter, or caufe to be entered, in the book belonging to their refpective parifh, and provided in purfuance of this act, all the infants under the age of *four years*, which, on the faid firft day of July, fhall be in the workhoufe, or workhoufes, hofpital or hofpitals, or other houfe or houfes, place or places, provided for the maintenance of the poor of each parifh refpectively, or under the care of the faid church-wardens or overfeers of the poor, with the times when they were received, their names, age, and whatever defcription re-lates to them, as far as can be traced, being agreeable to the fchedules annexed.

4. That from and after the faid firft day of July, all infants under the age of four years, who fhall be brought to any work-houfe, or hofpital houfe, or place provided for the maintenance of the poor, or be under the care of the faid churchwardens or overfeers of the poor, in their refpective parifhes, or any of them, fhall be, by the faid churchwardens or overfeers of the poor, or fome one or more of them, or by the direction or com-mand of fome one or more of them, entered regularly in the book aforefaid, with the times of their admittance, and all cir-cumftances relating to them, agreeable to the titles and heads of the columns in the faid fchedules mentioned and fet forth.

5. That the firft annual regifter hereby intended and directed to be kept, fhall commence on the faid firft day of July, and fhall end on the thirty firft day of December enfuing; and, after that time, the faid annual regifter fhall commence the firft day

of

of January, and end the thirty firſt day of December following.

6. That after the expiration of each year, the names of all the
infants under four years of age, then living and regiſtered in the
ſaid annual regiſters, and not diſcharged from being under the care
of the churchwardens or overſeers of the poor, ſhall be tranſ-
ferred to the regiſters for the year enſuing, under their proper
dates of reception, and under the deſcription in which they
ſtand in the preceding regiſters, previous to any further entry;
ſo that each *annual regiſter ſhall contain a full and diſtinct regiſter
of the whole number of infants under the age abovementioned,* under
the care of the pariſh that at time, as well as the children received under the ſaid age, in the current year, without being inter-
mixed or blended with the deaths or diſcharges of any in the
preceding years.

7. That the ſaid annual regiſters, and every of them, ſhall be
ſigned within thirty days after the expiration of each reſpective
year, by the veſtry, or any five of them, and by the churchwardens, overſeers, veſtry clerk, and maſter of the workhouſe,
for the time being; and where there is no veſtry or veſtry clerk,
by the churchwardens, overſeers, and maſter of the workhouſe;
and where there is no maſter of the workhouſe, by the churchwardens and overſeers of the poor.

8. That in caſe any infant is received into the workhouſe, or
under the care of the ſaid churchwardens or overſeers of the
poor, before the ſaid infant is baptized, or known to be baptized, due care ſhall be taken to baptize the ſame within fourteen days after the reception of ſuch infant, ſo that the chriſtian
and the true ſurname, if known, and, if not known, a ſurname

to

to be given by the churchwardens and overseers of the poor, or any one of them, be regularly entered in the said book; and the name and surname of such infant shall also be registered in the parish-register of such parish : and in case of a difficulty of distinguishing children, some proper mark shall be affixed to the child's cloaths, or hung round his or her neck.

9. That nothing herein contained shall extend, or be construed to extend, to such children whose parents receive money from the parish in aid of the maintenance and support of such children, they not being in the workhouse or other parish house.

10. That a copy of the said register wrote up, from time to time, shall, every month, be laid by the vestry clerk, or other person appointed for that purpose, before the respective vestries, or other parochial meetings assembled in vestry, that the same may be revised by them.

11. That the said copy of the register being completed at the end of the year, shall be deposited in the vestry-room, or other place or parochial meetings, to remain there for the use of the vestry-men, or other parochial meetings.

12. That the original register-book shall remain and be carefully preserved and kept with the rest of the parish-books in the hands of the parish-officers for the time being.

13. That all the respective parishes within the bills of mortality by the hand of their vestry-clerk, or, where there is no vestry-clerk, by the hands of the churchwardens, or one of them, shall, on or before the *fifteenth* day of February in every year, deliver fair copies of their respective registers of children under the age of four years, signed in manner hereby directed, into

the

the hands of the clerk of the mafter, wardens, and court of affiftants of the company of parifh-clerks, or fuch perfon as the faid
mafter, wardens, and court of affiftants of the faid company, fhall
appoint, he returning a receipt for the fame figned by himfelf.

14. That the faid clerk, or other perfon appointed by the
faid mafter, wardens, and court of affiftants of the faid company,
fhall receive the faid copies of regifters, and caufe the fame to
be bound in a book, collecting and ranging together the regifters
of the

    97 parifhes within the walls of the city of London,

    17 parifhes without the walls of the city of London,

    23 parifhes in Middlefex and Surry,

    10 parifhes in the city and liberty of Weftminfter,

in alphabetical order; and in this order he fhall, on or before
the 25th day of March in every year, make out, or caufe to
be made out, one general abftract of the fame.

15. That the faid regifters of the refpective parifhes, together
with the faid general abftract, being bound in a book together,
fhall remain depofited in the hands and cuftody of the faid
mafter, wardens, and court of affiftants of the faid company of
parifh-clerks.

16. That the faid clerk, or other perfon appointed by the
faid mafter, wardens, and court of affiftants of the faid company of parifh clerks, fhall print, or caufe to be printed, the faid
general abftract, and deliver fix copies thereof to every veftry-
clerk, or to one of the churchwardens, of all the refpective parifhes within the bills of mortality, for the ufe of the parifhioners
and parifh officers.

17. That for and in confideration of the expence and trouble
of receiving the faid copies of regifters, making an exact abftract
thereof,

(Schedule A)

ANNUAL REGISTER of the PARISH POOR (under Four Years of Age) from the [blank] Day of [blank] to the [blank] of the PARISH of [blank] (where there is a Workhouse) according to the Act of Parliament of the Second of His Majesty King GEORGE the Third.

Name of the Child. If a Founding, mark F. If a Bastard - - - B. If a Casualty - - - C. If the same Child is taken a Second Time, mark the Second Entry of the Name - - - 2. If a Third Time - - 3 &c.	Age real or reputed. Years Y. Months M. Days D.	If born in the Workhouse, when.	If not born in the Workhouse, when admitted.	Name of the Person by whom sent. If by an Officer, with any Child, mark the Name O. If by the Father F. If by the Mother M.	If Money be received with any Child, what Sum.	When died in the Workhouse.	When discharged from the Workhouse. If nursed by the Mother, mark M.	If Removed or Passed, to what Place.	When delivered from the Workhouse to the Father, Mother, or other Person. If to the Father, mark F. If to the Mother, M. If to any other Person, mention his or her Name.	Nurse's Name to whom delivered to be nursed. If a wet nurse, mark W. If a dry Nurse - - - D. If the Nurse dies, or is changed, write the Name of the new Nurse under the former.	Price of Nursing each Week.	Place where the Nurse lives.	Bounty to Nurses.	If died at Nurse, when.	If taken from Nurse, when. — If brought to the Workhouse, mark - - W. If delivered - to the Father - F. If to the Mother, mark - M. If to any other Person, mention his or her Name.

(Schedule B)

ANNUAL REGISTER of the PARISH POOR (under Four Years of Age) from the [blank] Day of [blank] to the [blank] of the PARISH of [blank] (where there is not a Workhouse) according to the Act of Parliament of the Second of His Majesty King GEORGE the Third.

Name of the Child. If a Founding, mark F. If a Bastard - - - B. If a Casualty - - - C. If the same Child is taken a Second Time, mark the Second Entry of the Name - - - 2. If a Third Time - - 3 &c.	Age real or reputed. Years Y. Months M. Days D.	When received under the Care of the Parish. - - - If born of a Mother under the Care of the Parish, mark the Date.	Name of the Person by whom sent. If by an Officer of the Parish, mark the Name O. If by the Father - - - F. If by the Mother - - - M	If Money be received with any Child, what Sum.	Name of the Person by whom the Child is received on the Parish Account.	If Removed or Passed, to what Place.	Nurse's Name to whom delivered to be nursed. If a wet Nurse, - - - W. If a dry Nurse, - - - D. If the Nurse dies, or changed, write the Name of the new Nurse under the former. If nursed by the Mother, - - - M.	Price of Nursing per Week.	Place where the Nurse lives.	Bounty to Nurses.	If died at Nurse, when.	When delivered to the Father, Mother, or other Person. If to the Father, mark F. If to the Mother, - M. If to any other Person, mention his or her Name.

And the Abstract formed since the Act, and digested for the Use of the Company of Parish Clerks stands thus, distinguishing the Divisions of the 97 within the Walls of London, the 17 without the Walls, the 20 in Middlesex and Surry, and the 10 in Westminster.

LONDON, [blank] YEAR

ABSTRACT of the ANNUAL REGISTERS of Parish Poor of and under Four Years of Age, in the [blank] Parishes

thereof, binding the regiſters and abſtracts in a book to remain as a depoſitary of the ſame, printing the general abſtract, diſtributing the copies thereof, with other contingent expences relating to the ſame, each pariſh ſhall, by the hands of the veſtry-clerk or churchwarden, pay into the hands of the clerk or other perſon appointed by the ſaid maſter, wardens, and court of aſſiſtants of the ſaid company of pariſh clerks, the ſum of fifteen ſhillings at the time the ſaid copies of regiſters are delivered to him, he paſſing a receipt for the ſame.

18. That if any churchwarden, overſeer of the poor, veſtry-man, clerk of the veſtry, maſter of the workhouſe, maſter or warden of ſuch company of pariſh-clerks, or any clerk of ſuch company, or any other perſon or perſons, ſhall neglect his duty as directed in and by this act, ſuch churchwarden, overſeer of the poor, clerk of the veſtry, or maſter of the workhouſe, maſter or warden of ſuch company of pariſh-clerks, or ſuch clerk of ſuch company, perſon or perſons, ſhall, for every offence, forfeit and pay to the informer the ſum of *forty ſhillings*; to be cecovered before any one of his Majeſty's juſtices of the peace, and to be levied by diſtreſs and ſale of the goods and chattels of the offender, by virtue of a warrant under the hand and ſeal of ſuch juſtice before whom the ſame ſhall be recovered, directed to any conſtable or other peace officer.

SECT.

S E C T. III.

REMARKS *on the* A C T.

1. **I** SHALL not forget when this Act was folliciting, that fome perfons of great note objected to it, as a thing unneceffary, prefuming the duty was already done; and that either there were no fuch evils exifting as the act fuppofed, or that it could not be a means to remedy them.——As to the *paft*, I had already examined all the regifters, fuch as they were, for ten years; and could not miftake as to the great point of neglect.--- And as to what was *to come*, time only could demonftrate.

2. The ample filent inftruction which thefe regifters contain, might well give occafion to the common people to call the act, *An Act for keeping Children alive :* and it gave occafion in fome pa- rifhes, to demand a higher price than formerly, with baftard children, tho' in fact nothing which can be reafonably de- manded, can be adequate to their fupport.

3. As the principal objects are the children under 12 months old, the *Abftract* fhould be rendered more particular in this point, and is fo far improvable, viz. at (*a*) may be inferted, *Of whom were under 12 months old;* and at (*b*) *Of whom were under 12 months old.*

4. By fuch parifh-regifters, as are kept with exactnefs, any child may be eafily traced out. And if they are not fo kept, I underftand that every officer in the parifh mentioned in the act, is fubject to the penalty directed by the law, for every offenee, which would amount to a confiderable fum.

18. By

By the article 18, the penalties clearly extend to church-wardens, overfeers, veftrymen, clerks of veftries, and mafters of workhoufes; and as the minifter generally makes one of the veftry, it behoves him more particularly to fee that juftice be done to thefe poor infants. It was prefumed, that the humanity of the clergy would induce them to lend a tender eye, and fee what is paffing, that there may not be any departure from the clear fenfe and commandment of the act, as well-knowing that the cries of fuch poor infants cannot eafily reach the lofty domes or palaces of Lords or Gentlemen, either in their private or legiflative capacities. They muft be informed, before they can redrefs; nor ought we to expect miracles, but a decent regard to humanity.

The 6th article provides that *each regifter fhall contain a full and diftinct regifter of the whole number of infants under four years old.*

It ought therefore to be clearly expreffed as a *title* at the head of each divifion in the regifter, though the fame fheet fhould contain the whole, viz. *Children transferred from the year to the year* , expreffing the date, fo that each regifter contain at leaft *four diftinctions of years;* and the *abftract* made by the company of parifh-clerks, to correfpond with thofe diftinctions, otherwife it is laborious to trace out the real ftate of things. This may create fome additional trouble to the parifh-clerks, for which they are paid, but none to the refpective parifhes.

Some of the *regifters* now mention the *years* in the column, with a *needlefs* repetition of them. The *title* above-mentioned would anfwer the purpofe more diftinctly.

D

Some of the regifters make no diftinction of one year's receipt from another, and confequently the children appear to be all of the fame year; and as if no transfer had been made.

2. In the general view of things, I now confider the abftract of 1765 as of fo many children received in that year, making however fuch diftinctions as hereafter mentioned.

Upon the face of the abftract of 1764, there appears to have been living, transferrable to 1765,

	In the Work-houfe and Parifh Houfes.	In the Country.
In St. Ann's Soho - - - - - - - - -	14	6
St. George's Hanover-fquare - - - -	26	14
St. James's Weftminfter - - - - - -	10	9
St. John and St. Margaret's - - - - -	26	8
St. Martin's in the Fields - - - - -	6	28
St. Clement's - - - - - - - - - -	1	
St. Mary's le Strand - - - - - - -	1	
St. Paul's Covent Garden - - - - -	0	2
The Precinct of the Savoy - - - - -	0	0
In the 10 Parifhes in Weftminfter - - -	84	67
97 Dittos within the Walls - - -	58	6
17 Dittos without the Walls - - -	119	1
23 Dittos in Middlefex and Surry - -	242	3
In all	503	77

So that thefe 503 and 77, in the feveral regifters of 1765, ought to ftand quite diftinct as fo many transferred from 1762, fo many from 1763, fo many from 1764: whereas there doth not appear diftinguifhed, by any date of year, near this number; confequently it becomes neceffary to trace the children *by name*, to fee if the identical ones are transferred, or dropt in the gulph of oblivion. This ought by no means to be the task of the enquirer. However, if all things were fair, and as they should be, in the great point of mortality, we might wink at some little inaccuracies.

3. Next year I hope we shall be better able to trace every one from the birth or reception, to a joyful scene of health and vigor in the pure air of some country village.—In the mean time, I hope the *vestry clerks* and others will do themselves the justice to conform to the plain sense and meaning of the act, in the circumstance above mentioned.

4. If it is really necessary for any of the officers of this year 1766, to raise their parish rates, as being otherwise incapable to provide country air, or other necessary things for the preservation of these poor babes, it is their duty, in the sight of God and man, to do it.

5. Those officers who think only of *shrouds* and *graves*, are enemies to their country, and may plainly perceive themselves to be in some danger. The indulgence shewn on this principle, that the office is troublesome, and without pay, will not be extended to screen them from the penalties of the law, for the non-observance of the *form* of the act prescribed; much less any scandalous neglect of the *substantial* end and design of it. Every good man in parish office will oppose such neglect.

6. Taking the registers and abstract simply on the face of them, even upon a comparative view of the common *bills of mortality*; and also of the mortality of the *Foundling Hospital*, when it was open, it discovers a vast field for enquiry, and warms the heart with the tenderest impulse of humanity.

The

7. The 9th article excludes *such children, whose parents receive money from the parish, in aid of the maintenance and support of such children, as are assisted out of the workhouse or parish house.* How many of such may notwithstanding, be included, when the mother is nurse, and sent out of the house, I know not. If a mother has lain-in, in a workhouse, or being in distress brings her child thither, and then takes it away again, and some weekly allowance is given her; in this case, I apprehend, there is so far from any violation of the act, that it is agreeable to the design of it, as well as correspondent with the good policy and humanity of the parish officer.

It is to be presumed, that many parish officers are excited to such acts of humanity, to avoid the *risk* of children's lives, especially those whose eyes are opened to behold, that *poor-houses,* or *workhouses,* are in general *slaughter-houses* to infants. The fact is, many such officers now prefer the giving assistance to mothers at their own homes, when in distress: if this method subjects the officer in some cases to be imposed on, yet of the *two evils* it is by far the least —It was thought, if it had been inserted in the *act,* to be included in the *register,* as if the infant were in the hands of the *officer* instead of the *mother's,* the parish might have appeared to save lives, which they had no other concern in, than by the assistance given the parent. I now think such assistance ought to be mentioned at the foot of the registers, that good parish officers may appear in the amiable light they are so justly entitled to; and receive the thanks of their fellow citizens, for the humane and honorable discharge of so essential a duty.

In

8. In the mean time, fome officers imagined the defign of the act was only to fee *what money was paid with baftard children.* This might make one laugh; but alas! it was natural for thofe who were confcious of a grofs abufe in this article, to entertain fuch a fufpicion. " The wicked fly when no man " purfueth."

9. With regard to the contempt which fome affect to fhew to the act, it was prefumed that it would meet this fate, tho' the the conditions of it are as gentle and perfwafive, as its bent and defign are humane. To have attempted much in the compulfive ftrain, might have been *unfair*, after fo many ages of relaxation of difcipline; but the time is come for a retrofpection, at leaft for a year or two. Some of the principal regifters, I am perfwaded are exact, but it may be neceffary that they be hereafter attefted upon oath to the beft of the knowledge and belief of thofe who fign to them.

SECT

S E C T. IV.

Obſervations on the Regiſter, and Abſtract of the Regiſter of the Infant Poor, with ſome comparative views with the Foundling Hoſpital.

THE abſtract of the regiſter of 1765, ſtands thus :

Born in workhouſes and pariſh houſes - -	463
Received under 3 months old - - - - -	170
12 months - - - - - - -	362
	995
18 months - - - - - - -	221
2 years - - - - - - -	96
3 years - - - - - - -	264
4 years - - - - - - -	219
	1795

Of whom were

Foundlings - - - - - -	115
Illegitimate - - - - - -	632
Caſual - - - - - - -	228
Legitimate - - - - - -	820
	1795

580 (as mentioned page 18.) being found to be living at the end of 1764, the real birth and receipt in 1765, is but 1215.

5   But

But in general, I will confider the whole 1795 as of the year 1765; the ages being diftinguifhed, it will make no material difference.

1. I remark how fhort the full number of 995 under 12 months old is of 4000 received in one year by the F. H. which I apprehend fhould have been confined to the relief of fuch children as thefe, and in fact took-in none above 12 months old.

2. The notion which prevailed, that only *illegitimate* children were brought to that hofpital, was erroneous. By this account, out of 1795 the number of 820 are *legitimate*, and 228 *cafual*, of which laft a great part may alfo be legitimate.

3. If 632 *illegitimate*, and 115 *Foundling* children, conftitute a number fufficient whereon to eftablifh a F. H. fuppofing a neceffity of performing a duty which fome parifhes are fo deficient in, the diftinction is obvious; they fhould be brought from fuch parifhes, fo unable to preferve them. For tho' in fome cafes, *amours* may be beft concealed, by a *fecret* reception of infants; yet if fuch fecrecy opens a door for numerous abufes, every one muft look to his own affairs. We fhould then know what we were about.

4. If a F. H. were eftablifhed for fuch Foundlings, what good would it anfwer, that may not be done as well *openly?* Tho' there will be always fome parents who chufe to give up their children for ever, others fhould not be therefore *tempted* by cuftom to give up *theirs*. The difficulty that arifes upon this, is, Can the parifh officers be induced to do their duty? If they can, is it not beft they fhould? In cafes wherein they cannot do it, fuch humane gentlemen as the managing governors of the F. H. may do

it

it for them. On the other hand, the fame good difpofition may lead Lords and Gentlemen to take care of their own parifhes, upon the foundation of the old laws, or *fome new one*, as in the cafe of the beft conducted parifhes, where the firft people in the land intereft themfelves. And may not a reafonable degree of zeal in a few perfons in each parifh, accomplifh all that can be expected, appealing to parliament for relief, where numbers afiect to dictate, if they commit any capital faults? No one body, *corporate* or not, can take proper care of all the infants in a kingdom : the idea is fantaftic, and experience proves the abfurdity of it.

5. It is very obvious that a great part of this kind of parifh poor infants, as are now in queftion, were faved by the F. H. in 1756 to 1760: but becaufe a defign is *good* in the degree, fhall we to run into the *extreme*, and make it *evil?*

I hope that vigorous efforts will be made to put this matter on its true foundation ; and that we fhall not wait till the old ftock, of children is run off, but that the Governors of it will *offer their fervice*, in the moft public manner, to relieve fuch parifhes as are in real *prefent diftrefs*, be they few or many. This will give them credit with Parliament.

7. From the number of foundlings being 115 (comprehending the remains of 1762, 1763, and 1764, though included in 1765) I conclude it is much lefs difficult to the human heart, and the dictates of *felf-prefervation*, to *drop* a child than to *kill* it. I conceive, that when murders are committed, it is to conceal fhame, and practifed at the firft moments of *delivery*, not afterwards, when the world knows of it. Therefore the good

2   which

which some so vehemently ascribed to the F. H. in this view, did not appear to me, granting its merit in many other respects.

8. As to the mortality of 1765, upon a comparative view, 141 were sent into the country to be nursed; of these were

Under 12 months old	74
Of whom died	32
which is per Cent.	48
From 12 months to 4 years old	67
Of these died	17
which, on 141, is per Cent.	12

9. This 48 per cent. is nearly the same number as were buried by the F. H.

10. These children, it is presumed, were born on the spot; many of the Foundlings were brought to the F. H. from a great distance.

11. These from their original stock must have been less the children of health, than those who were brought from the country to the F. H. And if such had not been brought, the mortality would probably have been 30 in 100 less, *i. e.* 18 per cent. instead of 48.

12. It must be observed also that what the parish officers call the *country* is within five miles of London; and that of 141 so sent, there are in this situation 120. It is probable a great improvement will be made in this article. Some of the most considerable parishes now send children into more distant places.

13. It is remarkable that a much greater proportion died of the children sent out to nurse, within this *small distance*, by the F. H, than of such as they sent into distant places, *i. e.* more

E

in

in proportion than the difference of ſtrong or weakly children amounted to.

14. We may alſo obſerve that the F. H. had conſiderably the advantage of the pariſhes with regard to inſpectors of nurſes; but this alſo eaſily admits of improvement.

15. Some of theſe pariſhes meaning to preſerve their children, pay as far as 3 s. a week for the nurſing, I ſuppoſe clothing included. The F. H. dropt their price in June 1756, from 3 s. to 2 s. 6 d. clothing excluded, but adding to the nurſe, whoſe foundling was alive 12 months after ſhe received it, 10 s.

16. The pariſhes find it difficult to get good and honeſt women as nurſes for their hundreds at 3 s. could it be expected the F. H. ſhould find good ones for 4000 infants, year upon year, for any price, unleſs they were *dry Nurſes* ?

17. The pariſhes want nurſes for 12 or 1400; the F. H. required nurſes annually for *four thouſand new children*.——Was this poſſible to be accompliſhed by *proper* wet nurſes, at a time when all the nobility and gentry, and almoſt all people in England who have money to ſpend, give up their children to be nurſed for hire ?

18. Notwithſtanding the fine airy ſituation of the F. H. in London, there was no ſafety even for 50 or 60 infants congregated only for a few days. Till they were ſent forward into the country they were always in the utmoſt danger. How can any pariſh-officer imagine he can preſerve infants in a *work-houſe* for a courſe of years ?

SECT.

S E C T. V.

Particular Inveſtigation of the Regiſters, and Abſtract of Regiſters of the Infant Pariſh Poor in 1764 and 1765.

1. **I** LAY it down as a general poſition, that the greateſt good fortune which can happen to a pariſh infant, falling into the hands of a workhouſe-keeper, is to be kept in it no longer than the F. H. kept them here in London, *i. e.* as a tranſit into the country.

2. If the mother is there with her child, ſhe ſhould for the ſake of it, remain no longer than to be *able to walk,* if not *to work,* otherwiſe the workhouſe that ſometimes *ſaves,* will in moſt caſes *deſtroy.*

3. Some few workhouſes are airy and ventilated; but in general the air is continually tainted. By congregating of infants they poiſon each other; and they periſh by this means, as well as for want of the breaſt and proper nutriment.

4. From the *ſpecimen* of pariſh officers *country nurſing,* as already ſhewn, there ſeems to be a diſpoſition in many to preſerve theſe infants, ſo far as they are pleaſed to extend this plan, which is *new* to them. But it muſt be obſerved, that as yet, no more than 8 in 100 have been ſent into the country as an experiment.

5. Some officers ſay they *can* preſerve children in *town,* as well as in the *country*: how do they make this appear, if they do

E 2

not

not try the *country* nurfing, and if it is a fact that they do not preferve them in town?

6. It requires fome time to enter fully and entirely into the *myftery* of preferving the lives of infants; and before the art is learnt, the humane and intelligent *officer* is changed. This would not be fo great a grievance, if mafters of workhoufes were better *chofen*; and fo paid as to make it the intereft of a man of fentiment, with a clerk under him, where a clerk is neceffary, to do the duty with tendernefs and circumfpection: good looking after may accomplifh this end.

7. We muft confider the ages of children in a *diftinct* view, to make fuch difcoveries of the *town account* of them, as will truly defcribe the nature of the cafe. We fhall then fee, that however hurtful an indifcriminate reception of infants may be in a F. H. in this nation, fuch an inftitution, within the bills of mortality, paid for, and fupported by the parifhes for whofe fervice it is intended, feems to be indifpenfably neceffary.

The merit of the feveral parifhes is fo different, it would be ab-furd to run thro' the whole comparifon; but we may take a view of fome particulars, and a general comparative furvey of the years 1764 and 1765, upon the face of the regifters, of which, I prefume, none are made *worfe than the truth*.

1764.

Parifhes.	Born and received.	Of whom living at the end of the year.	Living per Cent.
97 within the Walls	123	64	52
17 without the Walls	367	120	$32\frac{2}{3}$
25 Middlefex and Surry	735	245	$33\frac{1}{7}$
10 Weftminfter - -	468	151	$32\frac{1}{4}$
	1693		

Of

Of the 97 parifhes within the walls, I find

St. Stephen Coleman-ftreet has - - - - 6
St. Olave Hart-ftreet - - - - - - - - 8
St. Catharine Cree church - - - - - - 6
St. Martin Ludgate - - - - - - - - 5

Few others of the 97 have above one child, and 35 parifhes have not one, fo that it is eafy to reconcile their fuperiority in preferving life.

The number removed and delivered is 507, or 30 per cent. on the whole 1693.

9. But to comprehend the *good* or *evil* of this account it is neceffary to take a diftinct view of the children under 12 months old, *viz.*

Parifhes.	Born and received.	Dead.	Dead per cent.	Nurfed in the Country.	Of whom dead in the country.	Dead per cent. in the country.
97 within the Walls -	57	24	42	8	1	12½
17 without the Walls	188	76	40½	2	1	50
25 Middlefex and Surry	414	188	45½	6	2	33⅓
10 Weftminfter - -	281	104	37	98	22	22
	940					

10. Here we difcover that the inequality of the parifhes, turns in favor of the 10 laft, 5 or 6 per cent. on the *general birth* and receipt. This arifes in a great meafure from fending children into the *country*, and perhaps from their breathing a purer or *lefs poifonous* air in *town*. For upon thofe who are kept in town, and thofe fent into the country, there is a remarkable difference, *viz.*

	Dead per cent. in town.	Dead per Cent. in the country.
In the 10 parifhes in Weftminfter . .	37 .	. 22
In Middlefex and Surry	45 '	. 33

We

We alſo find that of 57 within the walls, have

had the fortune to be nurſed in the country   - -   8

In Middleſex and Surry, of 414, only   -   -   -   6

But the 10 pariſhes in Weſtminſter, have had the

honor of ſending, of 281   -   -   -   98

It is from conveying infants into the country that we muſt hope for the reſtoration of pariſh humanity.

11. Let us now take a ſurvey of the laſt year, in a comparative view, and try if we can diſcover any thing for the ſervice of theſe poor infants.

1765.

Pariſhes.	Born and received.	Of whom living at the end of the year.	Living per Cent.
97 within the Walls	102	63	61¼
17 without the Walls	377	118	31¼
25 Middleſex and Surry	821	330	40
10 Weſtminſter - - -	495	179	36
	1795		

12. This at firſt view diſcovers an advantage upon 1764; for in the 97, 25, and 10 diviſions, as above, there is a proportion of near 6 per cent. in life gained : the ages in general are not much higher than in 1764.

The number removed and delivered is 470, or 26 per cent. which is alſo 4 per cent. fewer than the year 1764.

13. In this year there are no leſs than 55 pariſhes *within* the walls who have no children at all ; from whence one may infer that they provide for the *mothers*, and leave them to take care of their own children ; or that the pariſhes are ſo rich the parents provide for their own infants, without any pariſh aids ; but I rather think the former to be true.

14. We

14. We fhall ftill be deficient in forming any adequate idea of what is *better* or *worfe*, till we take a view of infants under 12 months old, viz. in 1765, of whom there were 995.

Parifhes.	Born and re- ceived.	Dead.	Dead per Cent.	Nurfed in the country.	Of whom dead in the country.	Dead per cent. in the country.
97 within the Walls -	51	15	$29\frac{2}{3}$	—	—	—
17 without the Walls	196	85	$48\frac{1}{2}$	5	3	60
25 Middlefex and Surry	433	201	$46\frac{1}{2}$	5	2	40
10 Weftminfter - - -	315	143	$45\frac{1}{3}$	64	27	$42\frac{1}{3}$
	995					

15. Upon this it may be obferved as follows :

In 1764 the 97 parifhes *within* the walls, buried

a proportion of -   -   -   -   - $54\frac{1}{2}$ per cent.

And they fent into the country to be nurfed only 8 children.

In 1765, they fent none to the country, yet they

have taken fuch care, that the mortality is but $29\frac{2}{3}$ per cent.

At the fame time the numbers under 12 months old agree fo

far, that in 1764 it is 57, and in 1765, 51.

This is a *glorious faving*, let it arife from whatever caufe it

may !

It is remarkable that in the 17 *without* the walls, they have

buried in this proportion, viz.

In the country   -   -   -   -   -   -   -   60 per cent.

In town only   -   -   -   -   -   -   - $48\frac{1}{2}$

But the number of children being fo fmall as 5, there can be no judgment formed, except it be from the fame event having happened in 1764, the difference being 10 per cent. *againft* the country nurfing. From hence one may rationally infer one of thefe circumftances. This *country nurfing* is in fome places

2

lefs

leſs healthy than the houſes they ſend them to in *town*—that in town they are kept *ſingle*, and in the country *congregated*—or that they are in a dying condition when they are ſent into the country.

16. In the general view of 1765, it may alſo be obſerved, that there were nurſed in workhouſes and pariſh houſes, viz.

			dead.		per cent.
By mothers - - - - - -	613	-	250	-	$40\frac{5}{6}$
By nurſes in the ſame places - -	1138	-	336	-	$29\frac{1}{2}$

What proportion in workhouſes, and what in pariſh houſes, and what kind of houſes, and what ages the children were of, muſt be conſidered. There is much reaſona to conclude, that even the mother, *in* the bad air of a workhouſe, cannot preſerve her infant ſo well as the nurſe *out* of it. But here is no ambiguity, for $40\frac{5}{6}$ per cent. with regard to the age of infants under 12 months old, is much fewer than $29\frac{1}{2}$ of 2 or 3 years.

17. The common rate by the bills of mortality is $49\frac{1}{4}$ per cent. under 2 years, and but $11\frac{1}{2}$ between 2 and 5; conſequently we muſt conclude, that the *mothers* ſuckling their own infants, and only $40\frac{5}{6}$ per cent. dying under 12 months old, is ſo much *in favour* of the mothers, not *againſt* them.

We find even in the *country* nurſing in 1765, in Weſtminſter pariſhes $42\frac{1}{3}$ per cent. dead. But were theſe to continue in the workhouſe, they could not eſcape for twice $42\frac{1}{3}$, as I ſhall more particularly relate, when I come to diſplay the works of ſome particular pariſhes—The pariſh muſt have the credit of the care taken of the mother, but ſhe claims that of her child.

18. To take a farther view of the number of children under 12 months old, whereby to form the more juſt idea of what is

paſſing

paffing in the fields of infant blood, it is neceffary to trace out, as well by the *abftracts* of the regifters, as by the *regifters* them-felves, how many children, under the age of 12 months, were delivered or *difcharged* to mothers and friends; in the fame man-ner, as we have feen how many were *fent into the country* to be *nurfed*; and how many are *dead*. If we confider how fhort a time they live in the workhoufes, the number even of the *liv-ing*, under this age, in that *fituation*, will appear as it were with their *winding fheets* in their hands; I mean in thofe parifhes where fuch young children are not delivered either to their mothers or friends to be taken care of, nor fent into the country, nor yet given to fober women to be nurfed in town.

Of 995 under 12 months old, I find dead, either in the mo-ther's hands, or the nurfes, difcharged, fent into the country to nurfe, and remaining alive as follows:

Under 3 months old, dead - -	241 or $24\frac{1}{4}$ per cent.
6 Dittos - - - -	80 — $8\frac{1}{4}$
9 Dittos - - - -	50 — 5
12 Dittos - - - -	41 — 4

Dead - - - - - - -	412	$41\frac{1}{4}$
Delivered and difcharged to fathers, mo-thers, and friends, - - -	256 —	$25\frac{3}{4}$
Sent into the country to nurfe - -	141 —	14
So that of the 995 under 12 months old, (exclufive of the country nurfes) there remains alive in town - - -	186 —	$18\frac{3}{4}$
	995	

19. If we reckon the 186 on 598, (viz. the 412 and 186) it is 31 per cent. alive; but what a proportion of thefe fhall we compute will live 6 months longer? If we judge of the future year by the paft, not 10 per cent. will furvive 1766.

20. This makes it evident that the difeafe of inhumanity towards infants ftill exifts, and that the moft pitiable part of the human fpecies are yet in the utmoft diftrefs.

21. But on the other hand, the parifhes which have fent their infants into the country to be nurfed, exhibit a very different view, particularly St. Martin's in the Fields, whofe regifter in this refpect feems to figure higheft. Teddington, where this parifh fends feveral children, being a healthy fpot, and the nurfes there remarkably fober good women. The difference in the price of thefe and the nurfes of St. George's Hanover-fquare, I apprehend, is, that the latter pays 3s. and the nurfes find clothing; and the former 2s. 6d. and the parifh finds clothing.

Allowing for fuch errors as all fuch examinations are fubject to, the account ftands thus:

Parifhes.	Sent into the country to nurfe	Remain alive.	Under twelve months.	Remain alive under 12 months.	Rate per cent. alive under 12 months.	Rate per week nurfing.
St. Ann Soho – – _At Highgate 7, St. Michael's Berks, 1, Fulham 2, Whetftone 1._	11	7	6	4	66	2s. 3d.
St. George Hanover-fquare (a) – – –	35	23	22	11	50	3s. Cloaths included.
St. James Weftminfter _Batterfea, Lambeth, and Ifling-ton. The two laft places refemble London._	11	2	4	1	25	2s. 2s. 6d. and 3s.
St. John the Evangelift, and St. Margaret –	15	10	5	2	40	2s. 6d.

(a) See the Note page 35, oppofite.

Parishes.	Sent into the country to nurse	Remain alive.	Under twelve months.	Remain alive under 12 months.	Rate per cent. alive under 12 months.	Rate per week nursing.
St. Andrews & St. George the Martyr above Bars *Chiefly at Finchley.*	8	6	7	4	57	2s. 6d.
St. Martin in the Fields *Chiefly in Battersea, Tedding ton, Hammersmith, Chelsea. Brook-green, and Deptford.*	40	27	26	21	80¾	2s. 6d.
St. Paul Covent Garden *At Twickenham.*	6	4	5	3	60	—
St. Bride's Fleet-street *At Edmonton. There were 10, of whom 2 discharged.*	8	7	1	1	100	—
St. Botolph without Aldgate - - - *Not found in the Register, supposed a mistake.*	3	2	—	—	66⅓	—
St. Botolph without Bishopsgate - -	1	1	—	—	100	—
St. Peter Cornhill (of 4 years) - - -	1	1	—	—	100	—
St. Mary Aldermary	1	1	—	—	100	—
St. Dionis - -	1	1	—	—	100	—
	141	92	76	47		

(a) Places.	Sent to nurse.	Remaining alive.	Of whom under 12 months.	Remaining alive under 12 months.	Rate per cent. alive under 12 months.
Hammersmith - -	21	* 15	12	6	50
Hambleton - -	1	1	1	1	100
Wimbleton - - -	1	1	1	1	100
Lambeth - - -	3	* 1	2	1	50
Isleworth - - -	3	2	1	—	—
Padingswick - -	1	—	—	—	
North End - - -	3	1	3	1	33⅓
Kilburn - - - -	1	1	1	1	100
Edmonton - - -	1	1	1	1	100
	35	23	22	11	

* 3 of the *15 and the *1 are delivered discharged; so that in fact there are living in the hands of the parish-officers, of 31, 19 or 60 per cent.

and

22. By this account we may perceive that the rate of mortality is full 1 in 3 in the firſt year, forming ſome idea of the greater or leſs healthineſs of the ſeveral places near London, to which children are ſent. It will certainly be an improvement of this plan, if the children are ſent farther than *Lambeth, Batterſea, Iſlington, Hammerſmith,* or *Chelſea*; and this plan alone can regain the reputation of the pariſhes: this alone will ſtand the teſt of an examination; and all other attempts ſeem to be playing the fool with human life, and laughing over the groans of expiring infants.

23. Some pariſhes muſt be ſuppoſed more fortunate, ſome more careful, and ſome more judicious in their conduct than others: in every view, reaſon and common ſenſe plead for the *country nurſing.* But notwithſtanding all that can be done for theſe children in the firſt 4 years of life, if the pariſh officer is taken with a fit of parſimony, and then brings the child back to the workhouſe, he may near as well be taken with a fit of frenzy, and throw it into the Thames.—Experience teaches this; and if we have not yet melancholy leſſons enough on this head, nothing but ſome ſtrict legiſlative enquiry can open our eyes. And when all is done, if men of ſentiment and leiſure, want diligence and zeal, humanity or tenderneſs in behalf of *poor infants,* no *laws* can obtain the end in view.

and out of 22, under twelve months, 11, which is 50 per cent. And this rate per cent. on the few under twelve months old, ſent to *Hammerſmith,* &c. is as many as one would expect there, but ſhort of *Hampſhire* or *Oxfordſhire,* where, if my memory fails me not, this pariſh ſent their children in 1763, and why they now nurſe them ſo near London, I cannot tell.—This being a *pattern pariſh* it will be matter of the greater ſorrow, if ſuch Lords and Gentlemen are in want of *proper inſpectors* of nurſes in the country: *they* will not endevor to ſave *money* at the greater hazard of the *lives* of infants: nor can *they* fail in knowledge of the *value* of a life in a political or religious *view.*

24. We

24. We have feen by the bills of mortality (page 5.) that the common rate of deaths under 2 years old is $49\frac{1}{4}$ per cent. but from 2 to 5 years of age it is only $22\frac{1}{2}$ per cent.

25. In the abftract of 1765, the children paft 12 months old, are 800 ; and I find the account of them ftands thus :

Age.	Number.	Of whom dead.	Dead per. cent. on 800.
$1\frac{1}{2}$ year	221	71	$8\frac{7}{8}$
2 years	96	30	$3\frac{6}{8}$
3 years	264	58	$7\frac{2}{8}$
4 years	219	22	$2\frac{6}{8}$
	800	181	$22\frac{5}{8}$

This, at the firft view, might make one think that the mortality on 800 is but $22\frac{5}{8}$, or $2\frac{1}{8}$ per cent. more than in the bills of mortality. But when it is confidered that 204 have been difcharged (chiefly taken away with the mother at her breaft) the remains of 800 is 596, on which 181 dead are per cent. - - - - - - - - - - - $30\frac{1}{4}$

Whence it is apparent, that thefe parifh deaths exceed the

bills of mortality on the elder children, per cent. - $7\frac{3}{4}$

If we allow $\frac{3}{4}$ for the difference of $1\frac{1}{2}$ to 4 years old, compared with. 2 to 5, the difference is - - - 7

But if we mean to inveftigate our fubject, we muft examine the vaft difference of one parifh compared to another.

26. To redeem the reputation of parifh officers, and give nurfes an impreffion of a *real intention* to preferve children, it was hoped, the column in the regifter, " *Bounties paid to nurfes* " *as an encouragement to take all poffible care of the children*," would have produced fome effect. It was intended to be of the

nature

nature of a *premium,* and took its rife from a cuftom of the F. H. where, at the end of 12 months, 10*s.* was given to the nurfe whofe child was alive and well. This gratification being equal to a month's nurfing, made up in part for the *reduction* of the price, from 3*s.* to 2*s.* 6*d.* a week. How doth the parifh officer attend to this *tacit recommendation,* for there is nothing to be found in this column.

27. In the column, *Money received with children,* there is 1061*l.* 19*s.* 6*d.* upon 632 illegitimate children, which reckoned upon an average is 33 fhillings and 8 pence each. The common price is 5*l.* or 6*l.* and fometimes 10*l.* where any money is taken : but the number giving any money is but fmall, and this fum is fo little adequate to the fupport of a child, that the officers of one parifh, which I could mention, have ufually confumed or divided three quarters of the receipt in *expences of receiving;* exhibiting fo fhameful an account of parifh charges or expenditure of this money of the poor, as refle&ts difgrace on the very name of a *parifh officer;* tho' *a good parifh officer* is one of the moft honorable in civil fociety.

An obligation to pay *five pounds* for a lawlefs *amour,* will not reftrain the libertine part, even of the lower claffes of the people ; and I queftion if it ever brings about a marriage in thefe cities. With refpe&t to the children themfelves, it feems more confiftent that no money fhould be taken, unlefs it be paid into the hands of the treafurer of the parifh for the ufe of the children. As to *fadling the fpit,* as the feaft ufed to be called, it will *not give a day of life* to the infant : on the contrary, the cuftom of giving fmall fums feems to have introduced an opinion, that a *parifh child's* life is worth no more than 8 or 10 months purchafe ; and

that

that there is a chance of its being but fo many days, and confequently occafion a fpeedy releafe from all expence, and the
money may go in *good cheer*. Experience juftifies this fufpicion fo
far that the traffic of receiving money in fome inftances, feems
to be but a fmall remove from the price of innocent blood.

An acquaintance of mine, once follicited a parifh officer for
2 *s.* a week for a fervant during her lying-in, and nurfing her
child; alledging that a common parifh nurfe had at leaft that
fum, if not 2 *s.* 6 *d.* " Yes," fays the officer, " it is very true; but
" the young woman in queftion will moft probably preferve
" her child, whereas in the hands of our nurfes, after 5 or 6
" weeks we hear no more of them." This was a good reafon
with him, for giving more to the parifh nurfe than to another,
whom he thought would preferve her child. The deduction
from hence is too fhocking to mention. It is plain, *Cuftom*
will do any thing: and upon the fame principle, fuch an officer
will not be perfwaded to fend children into the country, nor
to the F. H. to be preferved, if he is to pay for the nurfing,
tho' it be with the parifh money. Sending them into the
country is the way to re-eftablifh the plan which our forefathers
fo judicioufly devifed for the relief and fupport of all the people
under circumftances the moft grievous to human nature

S E C T.

S E C T. VI.

Remarks on the Regifters of particular Parifhes.

1. HAVING thus inveftigated the *abftract* in a general view, I will corroborate what I advance, by a more particular detail of the account of *fome parifhes*, which have done well, compared with others whofe conduct feems to be fo bad, that *mercy* herfelf *pleads* for the *forfaken and diftreffed infant*, and demands redrefs.

2. In this view I prefent one complete regifter of St. George's Middlefex, which happily doth not contain a great number.—It fhews how defectively fome of the regifters are kept, compared with the *fchedules*, as appointed by law ; and what havoc is created by fome officers, in grofs violation of the duties of humanity, as well as the fpirit of the act of parliament.

REGISTER

REGISTER of St. George's Middlesex.

Name of the Child.	Age.			When admitted into the Workhouse.	By whom sent.	When dyed in the Workhouse.	Days lived.
	Yrs.	M.	D.				
Thomas Bailey -	2		—	2 Jan.	Overseers.	9 Jan.	7
Mary Bill - - -		2	—	4	Churchw.	17 Feb.	43
Elizabeth Bill -	1	11	—	4	Ditto	19 Feb.	45
Lucy Coleman -		5	—	24	Overseers.	11 Mar.	47
Isaac Darling - -	2	3	—	5 Feb.	Churchw.	13 Mar.	38
Ann Bailey - -	2	9	—	16	Overseers.	29 Feb.	13
James Gloves - -	2	4	—	20	Ditto	14 Mar.	23
John St. George F	2		—	21	Ditto	28 Mar.	35
Susannah Downes	2		—	4 Mar.	Ditto	15 Mar.	11
William Chope B		2	—	28	Ditto	14 Apr.	17
Mary Webb - -		8	—		Ditto		
Richard Yates - -		6	—	21 Nov.	Churchw.		
William Yates - -	2		—	21	Ditto	14 Dec.	24
Susannah Yates --		4	—	21	Ditto	21 Dec.	31
Jane Dryborough	3	9	—	22	Overseers.		
Elizabeth Hathaway	2		—	15 Dec.	Ditto		
Benjamin Tomkins	2	3	—	19	Ditto		
William Carns -	3	4	—	19	Ditto		
Peter Flidgard -	2		—	20	Churchw.		

Thomas Beal, Churchwarden.

This is a true and exact copy of the register of this parish of 1765, except the additional column of the days the children lived. If we consider the ages of these children, past the dangerous time of life, it is the more shocking picture of mortality; and the closer we approach it, the more ghastly it appears.

I have received exact information concerning the fortune of the *remaining* seven infants, which must be very interesting to those who think on the subject.

Mary Webb's mother has lain-in of another child in the workhouse since December last, and is happily escaped out with *both* her children.

G   *Elizabeth*

Eliabeth Hathaway is alfo taken out by her mother, and pre-ferved from the grave.

Peter Flidgard is likwife taken out alive.

Thefe three have efcaped, and fo far we muft give the pa-rifh credit. The two laft were but a little while in the work-houfe. The remainder are all dead fince December laft, viz.

		Years.		Months.
Jane Dryborough aged	-	3	-	9
Benjamin Tomkins - - -		2	-	9
William Carns - -		3	-	4
Richard Yates - -		2		

4. It is true that *man hath but a fhort time to live, and is cut down like a flower;* but thefe poor infants were mowed like grafs, for they had not fo many *days* of life in the workhoufe as the ordinary limitation of the *years* of man.

In the common courfe, not above $11\frac{1}{2}$ in a 100 of fuch fhould have dyed in a year; but, like a cruel eaftern blaft, the work-houfe has finifhed their lives, *not one* being faved from the grave, except the three fnatched from its gaping jaws by the mothers tender hand: nor could *thefe* have lived but by being watched and attended by the mothers, to plead for them with the *mafter* and managers of the workhoufe.

5. There is *no wonder* in this, when it is confidered, that thefe children were put into the hands of indigent, filthy, or decrepit women, three or four to one woman, and fometimes fleeping with them. The allowance of thefe women being fcanty, they are tempted to take part of the bread and milk intended for the poor infants. The child cries for *food,* and the nurfe beats it *becaufe* it cries. Thus with *blows, ftarving,* and *putrid air,* with

the

the additions of *lice*, *itch*, and *filthiness*, *he* soon receives his *quietus*; *our humanity* and *religion* are violated; and the *State* is wounded in its *vital* parts.

6. It is morally impoffible that infants can live under such circumftances. There are now in this workhoufe 100 men, and about 20 women; here are 200 *Poor* fometimes crowded together. This renders such places inevitable death to infants; and it is *confeffed*, without referve, to be a *rare thing* for a child to be taken *out alive*, except it be in the hands of the mother.

7. In looking back into this workhoufe account for the year 1764, I find 15 were received of thefe ages, *viz.*

8 under ———— 9 months.
1 ———— 1 year 6 months.
4 ———— 2 years.
2 ———— 3 years.
    Of thefe dyed in that year 13, viz.
7 under ———— 9 months old.
1 ———— 2 years.
2 ———— 3 years.
3 were delivered to the mother.
2 remained alive in the workhoufe:

Of thefe two there doth not appear to be any account whatfoever given.

8. I am farther to remark on this curious regifter, that *Tomkins* and *Carns* dyed of the *fmall-pox*, faid to be brought in by a poor woman and her child. Workhoufes feldom refufe objects, let the difeafe be what it will, if they are fent by two Juftices of the Peace, one of them being of the Quorum. I

pre-

prefume it is *very right* it fhould be fo, and that many muft
be taken care of under all circumftances, *i. e.* at the expence of
the parifh; but it feems to be *very wrong*, and contrary to common fenfe, and the fpirit and meaning of our Laws, that in-
fectious diftempers fhould be introduced into workhoufes, where
fuch numbers of all ages are congregated. On the contrary,
every one becoming fo difeafed, fhould be removed from it in
fuch manner as that the leaft mifchief poffible may be done.

9. As to poor *Dick Yates*, his brother William, and his fifter
Sufan, thefe were a *foldier's* children; their father had probably
ftood the fury of powder, ball, and bayonet; but inftead of
preferving his fons, in order to fupply his place, when time
fhall difable him, thefe poor boys died a miferable facrifice to
inhumanity and want of *police*.

10. This laft circumftance makes it proper to mention
that feveral humane gentlemen in the army, of the firft rank,
have now under confideration a plan for preventing foldiers children from falling a facrifice to indigence or vicioufnefs, or the
rigors that women are frequently expofed to in their marches and
change of place, with their hufbands (*a*).

11. I now proceed to the examination of fome other regifters.
One would wifh to be employed in difcovering the virtues of mankind, and to comment on the nobility of their nature: but it is
one proof of noblenefs to war with *petty tyranny* and *inhumanity*, and maintain the caufe of innocence. We muft feek
the enemy wherever he is to be found, and think it glory, even
if we fail in the attempt, to drive him out of his entrenchments.

(*a*) The States of the United Provinces, who underftand how to calculate the
value of a life, allow fo much to a foldier towards the fupport of every child, fuppofing his pay will only fupport himfelf, which is the cafe with us.

12. I

12. I believe the greatest *sink* of mortality in *these kingdoms*, if not on the face of the *whole earth*, is the united parish-workhouse of St. Giles's in the Fields and St. George's Bloomsbury, tho there are many opulent inhabitants in the parish.

Their REGISTER of 1765, stands thus:

Note, B. *Bastard*, C. *Casual*, P. *Parishioner*, F. *Foundling*; *The blank years, months, and days, are children born in the workhouse.*

Age.			Days in the work-house before death	Days living before discharged to mothers.	When received, being living at the end of the year.	Quality.	If nursed by mother m. if by nurses n.	Put out to nurse per week.
Y.	M.	D.						
I	2	—	28			P.	m.	
—	5	—	17			P.	m.	
—	2	—		140		P.		
2	—	—	46			C.		
I	—	—			13 Jan.	C.		
—	2	7	30			B.	m.	
—	—	—	14			B.		
—	6	—			15 Jan.	C.		
—	—	21	4			C.	m.	
—	—	—		27				
—	2	14	51			B.	n.	
—	—	—		22		B.	m.	
—	—	—		40		C.	m.	
3	—	—		27		C.	m.	
—	—	—		64		C.	m.	
3	—	—	11			C.	m.	
I	6	—	55			C.	n.	
2	3	—	157			C.	m.	
—	—	—	13			B.	m.	
2	3	—	20			C.	m.	
I	2	—		I		P.	m.	
—	—	14	25			C.	m.	
—	—	21	12			B.	m.	
—	—	14	2			P.	m.	
2	—	—	2			C	n.	
—	8	—			25 Feb.	B.	m.	1s. 6d.
2	—	—			26 Feb.	C.		
3	—	—		55		C.		
—	—	—			3 Mar.	C.		
—	7	—	70			C.	n.	
—	2	—			12 Mar.		m.	
—	—	14	7			F.	n.	
—	—	—	27			C.	m.	
2	14	—		4		P.	m.	
—	—	—	3			P.	m.	
—	—	—		24		C.	m.	

Age.			Days in the workhouse before death	Days living before discharged to mothers.	When received, being living at the end of the year.	Quality.	If nursed by mother m. if by nurses n.	Put out to nurse per week.
Y.	M.	D.						
—	—	—	—	24		P.	m.	—
2	7	—	—	—	23 Mar.	B.	—	2s.
—	10	—	99	—		B.	n.	
—	—	—	—	29		B.	m.	
1	6	—	—	1		B.		
—	7	—	—	28		B.	m.	
—	—	14	—	15		C.	m.	
—	7	—	—	55		P.	m.	
—	—	—	—	44		C.	m.	
1	5	—	—	—	3 May	P.		
—	10	—	—	18		C.	m.	
—	2	7	29	—		F.	n.	
3	2	—	99	—		P.	m.	
1	—	—	—	24		C.		
—	2	14	39	—		F.		
—	—	14	13	—		F.	n.	
—	1	21	—	27		P.		
—	—	—	—	63		B.	m.	
3	—	—	—	27		C.	m.	
—	—	—	2	—		C.	m.	
3	—	—	—	29		P.	m.	
—	—	21	12	—		P.	m.	
—	—	—	—	47		C.	m.	
—	3	—	34	—		F.	n.	
—	3	14	—	16		C.	m.	
2	—	—	—	21		P.	m.	
—	—	—	—	48		B.	m.	
—	6	—	—	10		B.	m.	
—	7	—	16	—		B.	m.	
—	1	14	20	—		P.	m.	
2	—	—	—	—	18 June	P.		
—	1	—	—	54		P.	m.	
1	2	—	—	12		C.	m.	
1	—	—	—	—	8 July	P.		
1	1	—	23	—		B.	n.	
—	5	—	—	4		B.	m.	
1	—	—	—	28		P.	m.	
—	—	—	—	20		C.	m.	
—	1	14	14	—		C.	m.	
—	—	—	—	17		C.	m.	
3	—	—	—	—	9 Aug.	C.	m.	
—	—	—	82	—		B.	m.	
—	—	—	—	24		P.	m.	
—	3	—	—	7		F.	m.	
—	1	—	6	—		F.	n.	
—	7	—	—	10		C.	m.	
—	—	—	—	30		P.	m.	
—	1	7	9	—		C.	m.	
—	5	—	—	13		C.	m.	

Age.			Days in the workhouse before death	Days living before discharged to mothers.	When received, being living at the end of the year.	Quality	If nursed by mother m. if by nurses n.	Put out to nurse at per week.
Y.	M.	D.						
1	—	—	—	2	—	C.	m.	
—	—	—	10	—	—	B.	m.	
—	7	7	3	—	—	C.	m.	
3	—	—	—	9	—	F.	F.	
2	—	—	—	—	25 Sept.	B.	—	
—	—	—	1	—	—	B.	m.	
—	—	—	15	—	—	C.	m.	
1	—	—	—	49	—	B.	m.	
—	2	7	—	5	—	C.	m.	
—	—	—	—	25	—	B.	m.	
1	—	—	41	—	—	B.	m.	
1	3	—	8	—	—	P.	m.	
—	4	—	—	1	—	F.	m.	
3	—	—	—	2	—	C.	m.	
1	—	—	9	—	—	C.	m.	
—	10	—	—	16	—	C.	m.	
—	1	—	1	—	—	B.	n.	
1	—	—	—	11	—	C.	m.	
—	—	—	—	—	25 Oct.	B.	—	
—	6	—	—	4	—	C.	m.	1s.
—	6	—	—	—	25 Oct.	B.	—	
—	6	—	—	6	—	P.	m.	
2	—	—	—	6	—	P.	m.	
—	—	7	5	—	—	C.	m.	
—	1	14	16	—	—	F.	n.	
—	—	7	1	—	—	C.	m.	
—	—	7	9	—	—	F.	n.	
1	—	—	—	8	—	C.	m.	
3	—	—	—	1	—	B.	m.	
—	—	—	3	—	—	C.	m.	
1	2	—	13	—	—	C.	m.	
2	—	—	35	—	—	C.	m.	
—	7	—	5	—	—	C.	n.	
—	—	—	20	—	—	—	m.	
3	—	—	—	—	11 Dec.	P.	—	
—	—	—	—	—	16 Dec.	—	—	
1	8	—	—	4	—	—	—	
—	8	—	1	—	—	C.	m.	
—	—	14	—	—	23 Dec.	F.	—	
—	—	—	—	—	24	F.	—	
1	6	—	—	—	26	B.	—	
1	—	—	—	—	26	C.	—	
3	—	—	—	—	27	P.	—	
2	—	—	—	—	28	P.	—	
—	9	—	—	—	28	C.	—	
—	—	11	—	—	29	C.	—	
1	—	—	—	—	31	F.	—	
—	1	21	—	—	30	C.	—	

13. The young man who came before the Roman fenate, being ftruck dumb with horror at the relation of his father's crimes, fucceeded better with the venerable fenators of Rome, than Cicero could have done with all his energic powers of elocution. But in fuch a cafe as this, is it poffible to refift the impulfe of indignation?—To behold in the feat of empire, in the very heart of a great and opulent nation, renowned for humanity, purity of religion, and the fupreme heights of literature, with every art of civilization: in fuch a place, to behold fuch an abode of complicated wretchednefs and mortality! Under the name of a *charity-houfe*, to fee a *flaughter-houfe*, to rob the neceffitous unwary parent of his deareft, perhaps his only property! How can the ftory be related in future times? Is there *no* remedy? Can *no* law be contrived, nor any interpofition be rendered effectual to make thefe *poor* cleanly, if not induftrious, or at leaft to fnatch infants out of the jaws of this *dirty* grave? Surely the thing is to be done, if we fet about it; or where is our boafted humanity?—When St. Andrew's above the Bars, and St. George the Martyr (not far removed as to their mortality) obtain the act they are now folliciting, we may hope it will be a prelude to fome reform of this fhocking parifh of St. Giles's. But to explain the regifter in a more comprehenfive view, I remark as follows:

By the 2d. column it appears, that the time allotted to thefe poor mortals, put into that workhoufe, from the birth to the age of four years, doth not generally, and upon a medium, exceed *forty days*. Were it not better they fhould die in the fweet air,

under

under the canopy of the heavens, and in this manner leave this earth, which affords them no better quarters.

By column 3d we learn, that thofe parents who venture to keep their children in the fame infernal region, longer than *forty days* on a medium, have nothing to expect for them but a grave.

Column 4th exhibits 26 living children, but 12 of thefe had not been received, upon a medium, above *five days*, and confe-quently no credit can be given the parifh on their account.

14. The whole account of this workhoufe of 1765 ftands thus:

Of 1762, 1763, and 1764, included in 1765, - 45 (*a*)

Born and received in 1765 - - - - - - 133 (*b*)
                                              ―――
                                              178

Of whom dead (Col. 2d) after a fhort life of   per Cent. on 133. (*b*)

       about a month   -   -   -   53 * -   40

Difcharged after a refidence in the mother's

       hands of near the fame time (Col. 3d) - 54 - 40$\frac{1}{3}$

Living, as far as appears, in the Workhoufe, - 14 * - 10$\frac{1}{3}$

Ditto received a few days before the year

       1765 expired (Col. 4th) -   -   -   12 -   9
                                              ―――
                                              133   Per Cent. on 45. (*z*)

Dead of the former years account - - - 8 - 17$\frac{3}{4}$

Difcharged of Ditto   -   -   -   - 8 - 17$\frac{3}{4}$

At nurfe of Ditto   -   -   -   - 6 - 13$\frac{1}{3}$

Living of Ditto, as far as appears by the re-

       gifter of the *three* former years, on about 260 - 23 - 51$\frac{1}{3}$
                                              ―――
                                              178

15. To calculate juſtly on the births and receipts of 1765, reſpecting the *inclination* or *ability* of the officers charged with this workhouſe to preſerve children, we muſt compute thus:

The *living* (as obſerved) may be called   -   -   14*

Which are per cent. on the 53* dead and 14 living - $20\frac{6}{7}$

or 1 in 5; but how long they can be ſuppoſed to live, no other habitation being provided for them than the workhouſe, is a propoſition that requires no deep reſearch.

16. As to the diſtinction of infants, in particular, under 12 months old, there are of theſe 81, of whom

			per cent.
Have been diſcharged to mothers, &c. -		32	40
Are dead - - - -		39	48
Remain alive - - - -		10	12

Of which 10, *five* were brought in within five days of the end of the year. So that with propriety we cannot compute more than *five alive* on the number of 44, (*viz.* the 39 dead and 5 living excluſive of thoſe diſcharged) which is $11\frac{1}{4}$ per cent. *living*. And what fortune will theſe $11\frac{1}{4}$ per cent. have better than the 39 who are gone to reſt? In a word, the whole ſervice done to the infants in this workhouſe, is to preſerve their parent, and ſuch as the mother takes out in five or ſix weeks: as for the reſt, it only gives them a quicker paſſage to eternity.

17. Let us return to the eaſtern parts of the town, and examine ſome of *their* accounts, and ſee if we can extract any knowledge towards preſerving the lives of infants.

St.

St. Mary Whitechapel.

Age.			Days in the workhouse before died.	Days in workhouse before discharged to mothers.	When born or received, living at the end of the year.	Quality.	If nursed by mothers M. by nurse N.	Price.
Yrs.	Mo.	Da.						
4					24 May	B.	N. Howe.	2 s. 6 d.
4					Septemb.			
4					June	F.		
3					October	C.		
4								
4								
4								
4						F.		
3			Nov. 23			C.		
2	6		- - - -	December		C.		
2			Novemb.	Novemb.		C.		
3								
1	6					C.		
4								
2								
2								
	7							
	6					C.		

Thefe children are all fent in by a parifh-officer—all received by a nurfe, whofe name is Howe, and nurfed at 2 s. 6 d. a week each. One may fee what wonderful things *may* be done by the regular payment of 2 s. 6 d. per week for children. Tho' thefe are paft the dangerous part of life, Nurfe Howe, wherever fhe lives, for it is not faid, is a notable woman, burying only 2 out of 18. But forafmuch as there are 7 without names, and inadvertently this account is not *figned*, I hope the officers will not be excufed paying the fine, if they trefpafs a fecond time. In the mean while, if the account is *genuine*, though they have neglected the *form*, they have obferved the *fubftance* fo well as to

H 2 be

be entitled to public thanks, and the higheft applaufe. I fhould think myfelf honored with their acquaintance. Their former account ftands thus:

Children.   Dead.

1762 they had 5, aged, 1, 3 mon. 1, 3 years, 3, 4 yrs. — 1

1763 ——— —— they are all difpofed of, or omitted, for the abftract is blank.

1764 —— 6, and *all living*; I prefume make part of the regifter of 1765.

This inclines one to believe, tho' they are fo carelefs in the ufe of ink and paper, they underftand what belongs to the duty of good citizens, and parifh-officers.

18. St. Mary Newington's account ftands thus:

Age.			When born or received. Born, b.	When dyed.	Qua-lity.
Yrs.	Mt.	D.			
1	3	--	- - - -	- - -	B.
--	--	--	9 Sept. b.	- - -	B.
--	--	--	5 Jan. b.	- - -	B.
--	11	--	- - - -	- - -	P.
--	--	--	28 March b.	- - -	B.
--	--	--	28 b.	- - -	C.
--	--	--	7 Septem.	- - -	C.
3	--	--	7	- - -	C.
	--	--	1 Dec. b.	19 Dec.	B.
--	--	--	1	- - -	B.

Here we fee a little parifh in the exterior parts of the town, acting with fo much caution and humanity, and probably with fome advantage in point of fituation, that in 10 children (6 being newly born, and 1 of 11 months) only 1 is dead, and it

gives

gives me the higher impreſſion that with the B. of the 28th of March 10*l.* is paid. Meſſrs. *Joſeph Fuller* and *Edward Ford,* churchwardens; Meſſrs. *James Pickering* and *Ralph Lowling,* overſeers; and Mr. *Lindſey Bull,* veſtry-clerk, I apprehend have acquitted themſelves well, and they will complete their duty as the beſt of citizens, and members of the community, if they will tell us who nurſed theſe children, and where; what they pay, and what rules their nurſes are under. Such a glorious account cannot be merely fortuitous! They ſhould take care, whilſt they are ſuch humane and fortunate friends to their country and mankind, not, at the ſame time, to violate the *laws* of their country by a neglect of what an *Act of Parliament* requires, according to the ſchedule annexed to it.——We do not uſually chaſtiſe any man, in this country, if he is fortunate: but it ſhould be remembered that the foundation of government is reverence for laws.

19. What reaſons there are in the nature of things why St. Luke's Middleſex ſhould not do as well as St. Mary Newington, or at leaſt as St. Mary Whitechapel, I know not. If the pariſhioners are poor and unable to pay, let them beg relief, for *God's ſake,* of private perſons, or of the *Legiſlators* of their country; but not loſe a life which they can ſave, and which belongs to the *public to ſave.* It is a ſhame to *national humanity,* that they ſhould die thus; and the wildeſt impolicy that ever entered the heart of man, to look on and permit ſuch devaſtation.

The

The account of St. Luke Middlesex stands thus:

Age.			When born, or received.	When died.	When discharged.	If nursed by mothers, m. if by nurses, n.	What price per week for nursing.	Quality.
Y.	M.	D.						
—	11	4		23 Jan.				B.
—	—	—	31 Jan.		11 Mar.	m.		B
—	2	14		19 Feb.		m.		
1	6	—		6		m.		
—	5/6	—		9		m.		B.
1	6	—	19 Feb.	16 May		m.		
—	—	8	19 Feb.	27 Feb.		m.		
—	—	15	9 Mar.	24 Mar.		m.		
—	4	—		29 Mar.		m.		
—	—	—	15 Mar.			m.		
—	1	—	24 Apr.			n.	— 6d.	B.
—	2	—	24 Apr.			n.		B.
—	5	—	29 Apr.	30 Sep.		n.		B.
1	9	—	8 May	3 Sep.		n.	—6d.	B.
—	5	—	24 May	20 Aug.		n.		B.
—	—	21	15 May			m.		
—	3	—	15 May	8 Aug.		m.		
—	—	—	31 May			m.		. B.
—	1	—	21 May		22 May			
1	2	—	1 June	19 June		m.		
—	—	—	25 June	{ 8 July		m.		
—	—	—	25 June	{ 8 July		m.		
—	—	—	2 Aug.			m.		
2	3	—	5 Aug.			n.		
2	8	—	15 Aug.			m.		
—	—	—	15 Aug.			m.		
—	1	—	26 Aug.	2 Sep.		m.		
1	1	—	27 Aug.	2 Sep.		m.		
—	—	20	15 Sep.	5 Oct.		m.		B.
—	—	13	17 Sep.	30 Sep.		m.		B.
—	—	—	9 Oct.		5 Nov.	m.		
—	6	—	22 Oct.	2 Nov.		n.		
—	1	—	21 Nov.			n.		F.
2	—	—	6 Dec.	23 Dec.		m.		
—	6	—	6 Dec.			m.		
—	6	—	9 Dec. 10l. given			n.	6d.	
1	—	14	9 Dec.			n.	6d.	B.
2	—	—	14 Dec.			n.		B.
1	6	—	18 Dec.			m.		
—	—	—	18 Dec.			m.		
2	—	—	23 Dec.			m.		
—	6	—	23 Dec.			m.		

Exclusive of the last month of December, here are 7 children above 12 months old, of whom 5, or $71\frac{1}{2}$ per cent. are dead; and

and under 12 months (26, deducting 3 discharged remains) 23, of whom 15, or 65 per cent. are dead, after a *very short life*; and yet these are said to be all nursed by the *mothers*, except 7; and to 4 of these *six-pence* a week are paid. Even this *douceur* of the poor fraction of a penny per diem, seems to be of consequence, at least 3 of these 4 are living. I have been witness to a worse account; but if their children, upon a medium of eighteen months old, do not live above *forty* days in *this workhouse*, it is much to be feared, before the *second* year expires, the *whole* account will be ballanced by *mortality*. I am the more suspicious, from knowing the particulars of this house some years since, and seeing that there is not yet any provision made for country nursing, or indeed any beyond the workhouse, where there can be no dependence made on any thing but the grave. By the several abstracts they had, born and received,

		Of whom remained alive at the end of the respective years under 12 months old.	Alive above 12 months.
In 1762	- - 40 - -	13 - - -	5
1763	- - - - -	13 - - -	3
1764	- - - 48 - - -	7 - - -	4

Of the last 7 and 4 no transfer appears to have been made into 1765, and consequently upon the face of the account there is a manifest violation of the law: but the worst is, it leaves room for suspicion, that *all* their children of one year finish their course before the next year expires; and that they chuse to drop them into the *gulph of oblivion*, that the account may draw a curtain over a part of the *horrid scene!*

Let us now examine another account.

5   St.

St. Mary's Rotherhithe ſtands thus :

Age.			Days in workhouſe before dyed.	Days in workhouſe before diſcharged.	When received, living at the end of the year.	Quality.	If nurſed by mothers m. if nurſes n.	Price of nurſing per week.
Yrs.	M.	D.						d.
1	—	—	of 1764. 131	— — —	— — —	C.	In workho. n.	10½
2	—	—	193	— — —	— — —	C.	n.	10½
—	6	--	153	— — —	— — —	C.	n.	10½
—	—	21	of 1765. 3	— — —	— — —	C.	— — —	
1	1	—	64	— — —	— — —	C.	m.	
2	—	—	—	— --	30 March	C.	n.	
—	—	1	3	— — —	— — —	C.	— — —	
—	—	1	83	— — —	— — —	B.	m.	
—	8	—	—	— --	8 April	C.	m.	
—	10	—	26	— — —	— — —	C.	m.	
—	—	1	— —	— —	15 June	B.	m.	
—	1	—	— —	— —	11 July	B.	m.	
—	—	12	7	— — —	— — —	B.	m.	
1	8	—	— —	— — —	13 Auguſt	B.	n.	
1	4	—	— —	— —	15	C.	n.	
2	—	—	— —	— --	7 Septem.	C.	m.	
—	8	—	— —	— —	19	C.	m.	
3	—	—	— —	— ʹ	23	C.	n.	
2	—	—	— —	— —	16 Novem.	C.	m.	
3	—	—	— —	— —	26 Decem.	C.	n.	

Upon a view of this account there is a clear transfer of 3 In the abſtract of 1764 there is made living 4. Upon a compariſon with St. George's Middleſex, it appears, that 10¼ d. a week will keep children alive, even *in a workhouſe,* above 100 days more than *no pay* at all. But, if it is *meant* to give them *fair play, half a crown* at leaſt muſt be paid *out of a workhouſe.* Here indeed are 11 alive out of 20, none being diſcharged ; whereas St. George's Middleſex has not one alive of 19 of the ſame ages (*i.e.* in 15 months) except the diſcharged. Of theſe 20, 10 were under 12 months old, of whom 4, or 40 per cent. were alive. Of the living I alſo remark, that 4 are illegitimate, of whom 3 are under 12 months old.

19. As

19. As I have mentioned St. Andrew's above Bars, and St. George the Martyr, to the fupport of which *I contribute my mite*, I am the more authorifed to plead for *their infant poor*. I hope my animadverfions on their regifter of the *laft year* will be of fervice to them in *this;* and that the difference will fhine forth to the honor of the gentlemen who intereft themfelves.

St. Andrew's above Bars, and St. George the Martyr.

Quality.	1 Age. (Y. M. D.)	2 When born or received.	3 Months & days before death in the workhoufe (M. / D.)	4 When difcharged to mothers or friends.	5. Where nurfed.	6 At what price per week.	7. Reduced price after 10 July 1765.	8 Time before death in nurfes hands. (Y. M. D.)
		1762						
B.	2 10 2	26 Feb.	— / —	—	Holborn.	3 s.	1 s.	2
B.	2 4 —	4 Sep.	— / —	—	Pear-tree court, Clerkenwell.	3 s.	—	2 4
B.	2 2 —	2 Nov	— / —	—	Puddle Dock.	3 s.	1 s.	
B.	2 — 13	20 Dec.	— / —	5 Nov.65	Finchley.	3 s.	1 s. 6 d.	
		1763						
B.	1 10 8	10 Feb.	— / —	—	Red-lion ftreet.	1 s. 6 d.	1 s.	
B.	1 8 24	7 Sept	— / —	—	Chancery-lane.	3 s.	1 s.	
B.	1 2 22	23 Nov	— / —	—	Fulwood's rents.	2 s. 6 d.	—	
		1764						
P.	2 3 9	22 Feb.	13 / 8	—		—	—	
B.	9 8	24 Mar.	— / —	—	Queen-ftr. Bloomfb	2 s.	—	
B.	2 — 4	28	— / —	—	Finchley.	3 s.	1 s.	
B.	3 8 23	17 April	— / —	—	Gray's-inn lane.	1 s. 6 d.	1 s.	
C.	1 1 24	8 May	— / —	—				
B.	11 12	20 June	— / —	—	Swain's lane.	3 s.	2 s. 6 d	
B.	1 4 11	5 Sept.	— / —	—	Finchley.	3 s.	2 s. 6 d	
B.	7 13	19	— / —	—	Baldwin's fquare.	3 s.	—	2 22
B.	9 11	21	10 / 4	—		—	—	
P.	3 4 9	23	— / —	27 Mar.65		—	—	
P.	5 6	26 Oct.	— / —	2 Jan. 65		—	—	
F.	2 18	5 Nov.	2 / 5			—	—	
B.	7 25	7	— / —	—	Finchley.	3 s	2 s. 6 d	
P.	1 22	10	— / —	2 Aug.65		—	—	
B.	1 19	13	— / —	—	Finchley.	3 s	—	
P.	1 3 16	16	9 / 7	—		—	—	1
F.	1 22	10 Dec.	1 / 21	—		—	—	
P.	3 20	20	2 /	—		—	—	

I

Quality.	Age.			When born or received.	Months & days before death in the workhouse.		When discharged to mothers or friends.	Where nursed.	At what price per week	Reduced price after 10 July 1765	Time before death in nurses hands.		
	Y.	M.	D.		M	D.					Y.	M.	D.
				1764									
B.	—	2	1	14 Dec.	1	1							
B.	—	1	9	14	1	13							
				1765									
B.	—	1	—	2 Jan.	—	15							
B.	—	—	—	3	1	12							
B.	—	—	—	6	—	10							
B.	—	—	—	6	—	14							
D.	—	—	—	8	—	13							
P	—	1	21	9	—	5							
B.	—	—	—	13	9	11							
B	—	1	—	15	—			Little Earl-street, Seven Dials.	2s. 6d				
F.	1	—	—	17	—	24							
P	—	8	—	17	2	9							
B.	—	2	7	19	—			Prince's-street, Moorfields.	3s.	2s. 6d.			
B.	—	9	—	19	1	6							
F.	—	1	14	27	2	4							
B.	—	—	—	31	—	15							
B.	—	—	—	2 Feb.	1	14							
B	—	—	—	6	—	10							
B.	—	—	—	7	—	9							
B.	—	—	—	11	—		6 March						
B.	—	—	—	17	1	17							
B.	1	2	—	20	—			Orange-street.	2s. 6d.				
B.	—	1	—	20	—	19							
B.	—	—	—	22	—	14							
P	3	—	—	25	—	20							
P.	2	6	—	25	—		25 Feb.						
P:	—	2	14	25	—		25 Feb.						
B.	—	—	—	27	—			Gray's-inn lane.	2s.				
P.	3	6	—	1 Mar.	—								
B.	2	—	—	2	—	14							
B.	—	5	—	2	—			Finchley.	3s.	2s. 6d.			
P.	—	—	—	3	—	12							
E.	—	—	18	4	1	24							
B.	2	7	—	9	—	26							
B.	2	7		12	—	17							
B	—	—	—	12	—	10							
B.	—	11	—	13	—	4							
F.	—	3	—	20	—	23							
P.	—	—	—	23	—		19 April						
B.	—	1	—	23	—			Hanwell.	2s. 6d				
B.	—	1	7	23	—	—		Pear-lane.	3s.	2s. 6d.			
B.	2	—	—	23	—			Feather-court.	2s.	1s.			
C.	—	9	16	25	—	23							
B.	2	—	—	30	1	5							

Quality.	1 Age.			2 When born or received.	3 Months & days before death in the workhouse		4 When discharged to mothers or friends.	5 Where nursed	6 At what price per week.	7 Reduced price after 10 July 1765.	8 Time before death in nurses hands.		
	Y.	M.	D		M.	D.					Y.	M.	D.
B.	2	—	—	30 Mar	1	5		Brown's Wells.	3s.	2s. 6d			
B.	3	—	—	30									
B.	—	6	—	1 Apr	—	17			—	—			
B.	—	2	—	1	—	18			—	—			
C.	2	—	—	2					—	—			
F.	—	2	—	4	—	9			—	—			
B.	—	—	—	5	—	10			—	—			
B.	—	—	11	5				Ormond Yard.	3s.	2s. 6d.			
B.	—	1	7	6				Islington.	2s.	—			
B.	—	—	—	9	—	16			—	—	—	—	16
B.	—	—	7	11	—	11			—	—			
P.	1	8	—	17	1	4			—	—			
F.	—	1	7	17	—	9			—	—			
B.	—	7	—	19	—	—	7 June		—	—			
B.	—	12		24	—	13			—	—			
B.	—	—	—	27	—	—	28 May		—	—			
C.	—	—	—	30			31		—	—			
B.	—	1	7	1 May	—	28			—	—			
P.	—	9	—	8	—	28			—	—			
B.	—	—	12	15	1	27			—	—			
P.	—	—	—	25	3	23			—	—			
B.	3	2	15	25	—	24			—	—			
B.	—	1	14	21 June	1	28			—	—			
B.	—	—	—	29	—	—	27 July		—	—			
B.	—	—	—	2 July	—	—	27		—	—			
P.	1	5	—	5	—	—	19		—	—			
B.	—	—	—	7	1	14			—	—			
B.	—	—	—	7	1	18		Brown's Wells.	2s. 6d.	—	—	3	—
B.	—	3	—	12					—	—			
P.	—	7	—	12	—	3			—	—			
F.	—	1	4	18	1	24			—	—			
P.	2	1	—	19	—	—	11 Sept.		—	—			
P.	—	10	—	19	—	—	19 July		—	—			
P.	2	1	1	19	—	—			—	—			
P.	2	6	—	24	1	18			—	—			
B.	—	—	21	24	—	8			—	—			
C.	2	—	—	24	1	21			—	—			
F.	—	—	1	2 Aug.	—	1			—	—			
C.	—	—	1	3	—	9			—	—			
B.	3	—	—	7	1	9			—	—			
B.	—	1	—	8	—	13			—	—			
B.	—	—	—	8	—	12			—	—			
F.	—	1	—	11	1	12			—	—			
P.	1	6	—	16	4	6			—	—			
B.	—	—	—	17		12			—	—			
B.	—	—	3	3 Sep.	—	9			—	—			
B.	—	2	14	11	1	15			—	—			
B.	—	2	—	11				Hanwell.	2s. 6d.	—			

Quality	1 Age.			2 When born or received.	3 Months & days before death in the workhouse.		4 When discharged to mothers and friends.	5 Where nursed.	6 At what price per week.	7 Reduced price after 10 July 1765.	8 Time before death in nurses hands.		
	Y.	M.	D.		M.	D.					Y.	M.	D.
C	—	—	1	13 Sep.	—	—	8 Oct.						
D	—	2	—	20	—	23							
B	—	6	—	25	—	23		Brown's Wells.	2s. 6d.				
B	—	—	7	26	—	23							
B	—	7	—	3 Oct.	—	29							
C	—	1	3	3	—	7							
P	2	4	—	4									
P	1	1	—	4									
B	1	—	—	5	—	13							
B	—	7	—	9				Aldermanbury postern.	2s.				
B	—	—	—	12	—	20							
B	-	—	—	30				Finchley.	2s. 6d.		—		7
B	—	6	—	8 Nov	1	—							
C	—	—	—	8	—	20							
R	—	—	1	23									
B	—	5	—	26				Finchley.	2s. 6d.				
B	—	2	—	28				Tash-street.	2s.				
B	—	1	1	2 Dec	—	—							
B	2	8	—	4	—	15							
P	—	—	—	10									
B	—	—	—	14	—	1							
B	—	7	—	14	—	10							
B	—	—	—	16									
P	6	—		28									
"	—	—	—	30	—	—							

OBSERVATIONS on the foregoing.

	Alive.	Reduced as per register of 1765, to	Of whom dead in 1765	Delivered in 1765.
In 1762 At the end of this year, tho' the abstract gives no account; this parish account being included in St. Andrew's Holborn, -	—	4	2	1
In 1763. The remains alive, agreeable to the *abstract*, were - -	26	3	—	—
The other 23 must be either *dead*, or *delivered*, in the *register* of 1764, which is not before me.				
In 1764. By the *abstract*, the remains are, - - - - -	26	20	10	
In 1765. By ditto, ditto, - -	37	—		3

Con-

Confequently we ftand in debt to this parifh for children nurfed by them, and brought in of 3 to 4 years old, being alive in their hands at the end of 1765, viz.

Of 1762   - - 1.

    1763   - - 3 of whom 2 are at nurfe at the price *of one fhilling* per week.

    1764   - - 20 are transferred to 1765, of whom 10 are dead in 1765.—3 are at nurfe in the country. 3 in town. 3 are difcharged, and 1 in the workhoufe.

Thus the remains of 1764, at the end of 1766, can be but 7, if they fhould have *all* the fortune to live!

In the year 1765 were *born* and *received* 114. How many of thefe are alive, and how long the dead ones lived, and where they died, and when others were delivered, appears by the detail I have given, the abftract of which detail is as follows:

From 1 to $3\frac{1}{2}$ years old	Of whom nurfed in workhoufes or not appear to be fent elfewhere.	Dead.	Days medium of life.	Nurfed by nurfes in town.	Dead.	Nurfed in the country.
24	17	10	32	4	1	—

From the birth to 12 months.	Of whom nurfed in the workhoufe.	Of whom dead.	Medium days of life.	Nurfed by nurfes in town.	Of whom dead.	Difcharged.	Nurfed in the country.	Of whom dead.
90	78	64	$24\frac{1}{3}$	9	1	11	6	2

Here we fee, of 24 of 1 to $3\frac{1}{2}$ years old, 17 nurfed in the workhoufe, of whom are dead 10, or per cent: $70\frac{3}{4}$

What aftonifhes more is, that thefe 10 did not live upon a medium above 32 days, *one excepted*, who

                      reached

reached 4 months and 6 days : and of the 7 furviving, 2 had not been a month in the houfe.

Whereas we fee by the force of 2 s. or 2 s. 6 d. a week in the *nurfes hands, even in town,* there is dead of thefe but 4 on 23, which is per cent. but   —   — $17\frac{1}{2}$

In regard to the children under *twelve months old,* of 90 poor infants, in fpite of experience and humanity, 78 are nurfed in the *workhoufe,* and of thefe are dead 64, or per cent.   ——   ——   ——   82 and they lived upon a medium 24 days and 8 hours, *only*—without the exception of more than *one,* who lived 9 months, 11 days.

At the fame time, where there is the expence of 2 s. 2 s. 6 d. or 3 s. a week for nurfing, there are dead upon 9, only 1, which is per cent. -   -   -   - $11\frac{1}{7}$

If the above account is *true,* thefe are fortunate *nurfes* and *favorite children;* for in the country 2 on 6 are dead, or per cent.   ——   ——   ——   —— $33\frac{1}{3}$

20. From the whole account it is evident that *cuftom* reconciles the moft barbarous and favage practices, and that thefe may pafs unnoticed in the moft enlightened ages of religion.

21. This parifh is now under confideration in parliament, not entirely on account of the *mortality* of children, which is not minutely known, but for other matters of oeconomical *police.* If it fhall pleafe heaven to put it under fome good direction, we may hope, whether the parifh rates be made *higher* or *lower,* whether adults eat bread of the fineft flour, or fome lefs milky white : whether they be fed with lumps of folid animal food, or good *meffes* in which a proper quantity of meat is ufed:

in

in any cafe, I truft the humanity of the *governors* will extend to the *poor infants*, as a valuable but diftreffed part of the human fpecies. I fay *governors*, becaufe I underftand thofe who may direct mean to be called fo; and 'tis probable the poor will fhew them more refpect under this name, than that of parifh-officers.

Churchwardens and *Overfeers* will ftill referve their name and office, but not an exclufive authority in the conduct of the poor, as appointed by the *old law*. This defect in the poors laws has often proved the bane of humanity. Indeed, where men of juft and tender fentiments are wanting, whatever *name* they are under, there mifery and diftrefs will abound.

On the other hand, *felect veftries* are confidered as monopolizers of parochial authority, and tempted to abufe it. The juft medium may be found in fuch perfons as are totally difinterefted, and capable of judging of the fitnefs of things, with candor and moderation, efpecially men of this clafs who have ferved in parifh-offices. Such governors may reftore fuch an equitable government as will content the reafonable part of mankind. As to the *poor adults*, it will not be eafy to pleafe the capricious, vicious, or lazy part of them; but judgment and candor, mixed with fteadinefs and mercy, cannot fail of obtaining all that ought to be expected in an undertaking of fome difficulty in the execution.

S E C T.

S E C T.   VII.

Further Reasons for a Parliamentary Enquiry into the State of the Infant Poor within the Bills of Mortality.

1. THE F. H. being shut in March 1760, I could not but weigh in my thoughts the *good* which had been done by it, though I had long deplored the evil. *This* was removed, but *that* was also taken away. It was easy to foresee that many of the parishes within the bills of mortality would revert to their old practices : I therefore determined to try to carry into execution, a design which I had formed in favor of the infant poor, sensible at the same time that the parishes in general would not heartily concur in any such measure. I was encouraged by the polite reception I met from the *Earl of Shaftesbury, Lord Ward,* the Rev. *Dr. Moss,* and other Lords and Gentlemen who interested themselves for the poor of the parish of *St. George's Hanover-square.* In my own parish of St. Martin's in the Fields, I also found several worthy and creditable tradesmen (*a*) two of them being my own relations composing

ing

(*a*) Mr. Richard Townsend, Woollen Draper to his Majesty, and Thomas Balack, Esq; one of the justices for Middlesex, and Linen Draper to the King. To the last of whom, in Feb. 1762, I wrote the following letter:

DEAR SIR,

It is with great joy I hear, that your present churchwardens and overseers, intend to send all the infant poor born in your workhouse, or brought to it, into

the

ing part of the veſtry; I communicated my ſentiments to them the more freely, and they gave me very high impreſſions of the

the country to be nurſed. The general complaint againſt you is, that you have ſuffered overſeers to take on themſelves to diſpoſe of infants arbitrarily as they pleaſe. But could it ever be conceived, that theſe officers, being *choſen by the pariſh*, under two juſtices of the peace (which pariſh your veſtry repreſents) ſhould *give laws to the pariſh?* And how it has entered the heart of any man, to recommend himſelf by parſimony, at the expence of the lives of his own ſpecies, when the *riches* of his country conſiſts chiefly in the numbers of working poor; is a circumſtance which the moſt barbarous ages could never have any conception of.

Never ſurely was a more capital blunder committed in any civilized ſtate, or any Chriſtian country, than the doctrine of ſaving money to the pariſh, by ſuffering the infant poor to die! The pariſh is a part of the community in the ſame manner, though in a greater degree, as a private family is part of it. A number of private families conſtitute a pariſh, and ſupport their own poor, not the poor of other pariſhes; and you will ſee by the calculation incloſed, which is thought to be a modeſt one, that every child who dies, inſtead of being a *ſaving*, creates a *loſs*, or prevents a gain, to the community of 184*l.* 3*s.* 3*d.*

Sad experience for *half* a century, or a *whole* one as far as I know, has taught, that though it is certain deſtruction to infants to leave them to be nurſed in your workhouſes, or in places where numbers of adults are congregated, yet it has been continued, and the pariſhioners have been careleſs ſpectators.

To truſt the lives of infants, as is generally done, in the hands of perſons whoſe very ſituation in the workhouſe, in general, implies their being either careleſs or indolent, ſickly or inſane, ſtupid, abandoned, or ſuperannuated, is ſhocking to humanity and common policy.

I have attended the deaths of near ten thouſand children, out of 15000, who have been received by order of parliament in the Foundling Hoſpital; and I know too well how the effects of the vices of the common people, particularly in theſe great cities, extend to their offspring: but for the ſame reaſon that common proſtitution creates ſterility, the number of children born diſeaſed, I apprehend is not near ſo large as ſome pariſh-officers would have it thought.

As to illegitimate children and foundlings, they are for the moſt part born of domeſtic ſervants, and begotten in the warmth of good ale, beef, and pudding:

K

the

the gentlemen who compofed their veſtry. I have related what a happy change the pariſh-officers have made in their pariſh,

the death of ſuch infants is therefore the more capital reproach. Children who are in the medium between theſe two extremes, ought, on the great principles of policy and humanity, to have as fair a chance of life as the children of peers of the realm ; and it would be ſo, but that policy and humanity have been long out of faſhion in pariſh governments. The evil has been long complained of, and no remedy found but the Foundling Hoſpital, and this has proved as bad as the diſeaſe.

We are now endevoring to reſtore things to their primitive ſtate, and by the bleſſings of heaven, repair the havoc of workhouſes as well as of the field. The deſign of a regular uniform regiſter will probably operate in this manner. It will be moſt truly honorable for the *King's pariſh* to take the lead, and the names of your veſtry, and the preſent churchwardens and overſeers, will deſerve to be tranſmitted down to poſterity with the higheſt commendations.

If you purſue the plan propoſed, of giving good premiums to nurſes who preſerve the children you commit to their care (which was practiced with ſucceſs by the Foundling Hoſpital) you will make it the intereſt and the honor of the nurſes to ſave the children ; or if you chuſe good women as nurſes, and pay them properly, you will turn the current of the bad opinion prevailing among the common people, namely, *that pariſh officers never intend that pariſh infants ſhould live.*

In the mean while I recommend to your caution, to diſtinguiſh healthy children from diſeaſed, eſpecially ſuch as may have any venereal taints. You have greatly the advantage of the Foundling Hoſpital, becauſe you know the parents, and can judge from thence of the ſtate of the child ; but if the wife of the maſter of your workhouſe, or any other woman having common ſenſe, is taught to examine and make the diſtinction ; or if you have a medical gentleman to examine your children when you ſend them to nurſe, and diſtinguiſh the clean from the foul, or the ſuſpected, you will then breed the two latter by hand, and not run any riſk of hurting a nurſe, which but very rarely happens. This will give your children a reputation among nurſes, and you a title to examine alſo into the ſtate of the health of nurſes, that no child be hurt by any of *them,* which is by far the more probable caſe.

Moreover

rifh, where the devaftation of infants had been formerly full as great as in any other.

2. In 1761 I examined the regifters of all the parifhes, from 1750 to 1755 inclufive, and I found that the *deaths* and *difcharges* nearly

Moreover when you cannot find good wet nurfes, and are obliged to wean children, I am told, and I have feen fome inftances, that females are in lefs danger without the breaft than males ; but this I muft refer to the learned, remembering that in the view of population, the female is the moft valuable. The order of Nature is the breaft. The common deviation from it by women giving their children up to others to be fuckled, makes it almoft impoffible that all the children of the poor can be properly nourifhed ; but it fhould ever be remembered, that the breaft even for a month, a week, or a day, may frequently fave a life. And upon the whole, the more you encourage women who are not abandoned, to fuckle their own children, the better it will be.

If you mean to have your children bred to be ftrong, ufeful, and virtuous, do not bring them back to London from their nurfes in the country. If you really mean to *preferve their lives*, never think them fafe in a workhoufe. Keep them where they are well ; 'prentice them out there, and let London be recruited by ftrong people, who have imbibed good fentiments. In any cafe, remember that fweet air is the balm of life ; and how thefe young perfons can partake of it freely, when mixed with the filthy or difeafed, the old or infirm, or with any great number of adults, in any place, much more in fuch rooms as workhoufes afford, is above my comprehenfion. It is the fafhion of the times to love a *crowd*, but the fmaller the number you bring together, old or young, fick or well, you may be affured the more healthy they will be. I heartily wifh you fuccefs, and am, with great truth,

Dear Sir,

Your moft obedient,

and affectionate fervant.

JONAS HANWAY.

nearly made up the whole hiſtory of the lives of the pariſh infant poor. And theſe *diſcharges* ſeldom meant more than a delivery to the mother, after a few days or weeks reſidence. To mention fourteen of the moſt conſiderable, their ſix years account abovementioned ſtands thus :

Pariſhes.	Born and received.	Diſcharged.	Dead.	Remain alive in 1755.
St. George Hanover-ſquare *One of the beſt.*	288	115	137	36
St. Luke, Middleſex - - *The worſt, no one eſcaping through the whole year.*	53	——	53	——
St. Giles's in the Fields, and St. George's Bloomſbury - *Very bad.*	415	228	169	18
St. Andrew's above Bars, and St. George the Martyr - *No better.*	284	57	222	5
St. Ann Weſtminſter - - *Now much improved.*	66	30	28	8
St. Saviour's Southwark -	156	91	56	9
St. Paul's Shadwell - - -	32	11	12	9
St. Martin's in the Fields - *Now ſo much mended.*	312	147	158	7
St. Margaret and St. John, Weſtminſter - - -	129	32	68	29
Lambeth - - -	76	53	23	——
Chriſt Church, Surry -	39	19	18	2
St. Giles without Cripplegate	209	131	62	16
St. Botolph without Aldgate	119	57	33	29
St. James Weſtminſter -	161	103	58	——

3. Theſe

3. Thefe fmall remains being followed into the year 1756, it is probable we fhould find they had the fame fate as their predeceffors. Thofe who furvived till June, in that year, were conveyed to the F. H. then open for an indifcriminate reception; in confequence of which, *one* life in *three* has been faved. Whether the health of the *country children*, under the difadvantage of being brought a journey, was more than counterbalanced by the difeafes of the *town children*, (many of which were brought reeking from the womb) fo as to form a judgment, if the living children are moftly of the town or country produce, is a matter that will remain undecided.

4. From this view of 6 years, it may be prefumed, that for ages before the opening of the F. H. *for fuch general reception*, the parifh officers within the bills of mortality, fported away the lives of many thoufand children. They acknowledged that a very inconfiderable number of thofe born in workhoufes, or brought to them in infancy, were ever reared, and that the pious and politic intention of our good forefathers, were in this inftance defeated. In fact, the office of an elder of the parifh, a father of the poor, *viz.* a church-warden, or overfeer of the poor, with refpect to the moft helplefs of mankind, was become a cruel exercife of authority, the officer acting as the wolf toward the lamb in the fable. If the child brought money, it was fquandered, or deemed no object: if no money was brought, this was a *fecret* reafon why no expence fhould be made upon it; and in either cafe the child became a facrifice.

5. I hope it will be agreeable to the wifdom of the legiflature, to call for the *abftract* of the regifters, in order to an enquiry

quiry into *the regiſters themſelves*, and in due time to examine into the hard fortune of this claſs of his majeſty's ſubjects, upon the foundation of the act of parliament for the regiſters.

If the life of one ſubject is as ſacred as that of another, and no life can be loſt without ſolemn inquiſition, ſurely the whole ſtrength of legiſlation will interpoſe in defence of ſo many thouſands of ſuch innocent children as the courſe of years produces. And wherever there is an apparent want of knowledge or humanity, ſo that it is evident *no perſwaſive law* can operate, it may be preſumed, that a *compulſive* obligation will take place; at the ſame time that a due attention is paid to the pecuniary abilities and ſituation of individuals, that whilſt we are in purſuit of mercy to children, we may commit no act of cruelty to men. Retroſpections in theſe caſes, anſwer as leſſons of inſtruction for future conduct: but beyond this, in ſuch mutable bodies, it would be a vain enquiry.

6. I have in ſeveral places mentioned, how groſsly ſome of the pariſh accounts deviate from the act for the *regiſter*, as if the officers imagined no one would take any cognizance of their conduct. Whether all have committed their tranſactions in relation to theſe children to writing, even in their own books, is a queſtion they can beſt anſwer.

7. Theſe gentlemen ſhould reflect, that whatever vulgar notions are entertained concerning *informations*, ſome breaches of laws proclaim themſelves; and this is one of that kind. Moreover it will be *mercy* to the infant, not *malice* to them, which may induce any one to enter a legal, formal information, in a matter of ſo ſerious a nature.

After

After making good laws for the welfare of the community, the maintaining and preferving them from violation ought to be held next in rank and eftimation. And when the *good* officer fees any one neglect his duty, he will be the firft to cry for *mercy* on the infant. My motives as a *fubject*, a *citizen*, or a *chriftian*, ought to be common; but I am alfo in a habit of thinking of fuch objects, from being converfant with them, and that my relation to them as a man, is ftronger than any I bear to thofe who ftand in no need of any help from me.

8. If thefe poor babes could tell how cruelly they have been treated, the very ftones (as was once faid on a more important occafion) would cry out againft the offenders.—If we feel for *liberty*, are not the rights of children as *facred* as any other? If we confider things in a religious view, is not man formed by his almighty creator for the prefervation his own fpecies: and are we not prompted to confult how beft to preferve and fupport our fellow creatures? Do we not *depend* on the poor, as well as as they on us? Do not our reafon and affections unite to this common end?—If a parifh child may be fuffered to perifh for want of the neceffaries of life, fo may any other child. But the Almighty has promifed his rewards, and threatened his punifhments, for our neglect in the exercife of mercy and com-paffion: are thefe poor babes excluded the divine philanthropy? On the contrary, are we not perpetually reminded of the poor, as if the great parent of mankind, our common father, is their more immediate friend and protector.

Cuftom may render us more favage than thofe Indians who are faid to offer up their children as facrifices to their *deities*. They *kill* one now and then with a knife, or other inftrument: is not

2   this

this lefs barbarous than *ftarving, over-laying,* or *lingering difeafes,* contracted by fleeping with filthy, unhealthy perfons, or breathing putrid air.

Nor do we mean to wink at a cuftom lefs civilized than that of China. The *Pagan Chinefe,* I am told, may legally drown their female children, but they feldom take any advantage of the law. Nature wars againft it ; but an Englifh churchwarden or overfeer of the poor, within the bills of mortality, under the fanction of his office, may fuffer children to be ftarved to death, or poifoned with noxious air. Cuftom authorifes the practife, and he may go on in it from generation to generation ; he may *do* all he can to *undo* his country, and yet pafs with impunity !

9. In a political view, it is univerfally affented to, that the number of the working people (who muft be *poor,* or they would not work) conftitute the ftrength, opulence, and capacity of defence in a nation.—In the fame view, may we not confider a child as we do a *calf,* a *lamb,* or a *colt ?* They being fo much lefs noble animals, are fooner reared, and are of fome ufe, particularly the two former, for their fkins and flefh, foon after they have feen the light. But if they are kept for their proper benefit of milk, flefh, and fkin, and the generous horfe for his fervice, we compute that they will *repay* the charge. In the fame manner, it is grofs ignorance of the value of a human life, that makes us fo carelefs about the infant parifh poor.

10. Let us compute the value of a life in the mercantile ftate of profit and lofs.

The charge of a parifh, or any other poor child, I fuppofe to be in the 3 firft years of life, at 3*s.* per week, clothing and all

2   included

	£.	s.	d.
included (in the country) - - - -	23	8	0
4 next years, ditto, at 2 s. 6 d, per week, -	26	0	0
6 next years (taking in the produce of his labor, if he is put in any train of life,) cannot be above 1 s. per week, - - - -	15	12	0

I suppose that 2 in 5 may, with decent care, be reared; and that much the greatest mortality is in the first year, and the next 18 months. Putting this at a high computation of expence, to supply the mortality which may happen after $2\frac{1}{2}$ years, we may reckon thus :

	£.	s.	d.
A child one whole year, at 3 s. a week dead, -	7	16	0
$\frac{1}{2}$ a child (which makes it equal to 2 in 5 saved) on a medium of 4 years at 2 s. 6 d. dead -	13	0	0
	85	16	0

11. Now let us see if the *farmer* or *manufacturer*, the *baker*, *brewer*, *cook*, *butcher*, or *taylor*, or any trade essential to life, were to pay for the support of such child, boy or girl, so brought up to the age of 13,—what would he or she render him? We may compute the medium of life fit for labor, to be till 36, years of age. Some die more early; some become sickly, and some are stout till *fifty* or *three-score*. If we take the medium of life, for labor, to be 36 years, then there is 23 years service, after the age of 13. 23 Years at the computation of *nine-pence*, value of labor gained for both

	£.	s.	d.
sexes, (Sundays excepted) amounts to - -	269	19	3
Deduct the charge, as mentioned, of - -	85	16	0
And there is a gain of - - - - -	184	3	3

L

If

If the experiment were tried, it is more than probable the mafter, if he hoarded the gains of a good fervant for 23 years, would find himfelf at leaft fo much in pocket. We are to compute, that 9 pence a day is nearly 11*l*. 15*s*. per ann. which on 4 millions of people (out of 7 millions fuppofed to be at work) makes   -   -   -   -   -   -   47,000,000   o   o
And if we eftimate the real expences of rich and poor, young and old, at 6*l*. 14*s*. 6*d*. each, it comes to   -   -   -   -   -   47,075,000   o   o
This in fome meafure fupports the analogy of the computation. I reckon 7*l*. 16*s*. even for a parifh child for the firft danger-ous year of life; but this is the *pay*, and part of the fupport of the nurfe as well as the child; and if the labor of 23 years is fet at its full value, fo is the charge of childhood.

12. With refpect to the conduct of the parifh officers in queftion, an Englifhman furely never meant to be *cruel*; it is againft his nature, it is againft his genius and turn of mind. The officers themfelves, who thus tranfgrefs, *mean no harm:* they only *fuffer* it by *the force of cuftom*. It is want of confidering the value of a life, it is a miftake with regard to duty. They know there is *fomething to be faved*, but they miftake the object; they fave the *money* when they fhould fave the *life*. They may not comprehend, that if his majefty had twice as many fubjects as he has, there would be the more riches in the country. Find employment of fome kind or other, and there is no danger of our being over-run with numbers.—But in any cafe, I hope they will no longer think of faving the *money*,

and

and lofing the *life*, more than they would *gain* the *world* and *lofe* their *fouls*. If the fhedding of innocent blood is a fin of the blackeft dye, whatever appears *indifferent, whether a child lives or not*, has fomething in it that is *horrible*. And if, by a cruel exaction of *unneceffary hardfhips*, we may deftroy a man, more eafily may we, by cruelly *with-holding* what is *a neceffary provifion*, deftroy *a child*. I hope they will think of thefe things, and that in confequence of it, the choiceft bleffings will attend them.

13. Let what will be done by the F. H. in relief of the infant poor in diftrefs, upon the principle of the propofal that follows, to form a juft idea of what is paffing in parifhes in relation to young perfons, (who are the moft valuable of any taken into workhoufes) the parifh officers ought to account for children fomewhere, for thefe cannot plead their own caufe. My fpe-culation regards children only, and I would follow them clofe from the womb, till they are placed out in the world; that juftice may be done them.

14. To call for the abftracts of the regifters may be enough for the *prefent*, but hereafter I fhould rejoice to hear a refolution of the H. of C. that each parifh refpectively, within the bills of mortality, fhall annually give a diftinct account, according to a form prefcribed, of the name, time when born or received, age when placed out, to whom placed, where living, what trade, what money given, and other particulars, of every child the parifh places out in the year. This might be a means of com-pleting a work which the regifter leaves imperfect.

S E C T.

SECT. VIII.

Proposal for sending all Children under four years old to the F. H.
*from such parishes as appear unable or unwilling to preserve them;
the same to be done upon terms to be agreed.*

1. IT is in vain to consider the value of any thing, if we must
part with it before it is fit for use or ornament.—Upon
the same principle, if there are parishes incapable of preserving the lives of children, from whatever cause it may arise, *they*
ought in all reason to look out for some effectual assistance, and
if *they* do not, those who are spectators, and mean to do good
or prevent evil, must do it for them.

2. Considering what numbers of children there are, whose
mothers are dead, or lost to them, in these great cities, or
grown vicious and unfit to be trusted with their own children;
or the child, being illegitimate, it may not in all cases be
conveniently shewn to the world: If the mother is in distress
for bread, or used to a better air than is found in a workhouse, and therefore finds it next to death to be in a workhouse, or is ashamed to throw herself, with her child, on charity :
Considering also, how many *Foundlings* there are, whose mothers
are totally concealed: In these various circumstances, if some
provision is not made, more effectual than many parishes now
provide, in the eye of humanity and religion, the land must
weep, if it is not in too strong a sense *stained* with infant blood.

4

3. So

3. So far the matter refts on the fame foundation as in the time of Capt. *Coram*, who feemed to have too diffufe an idea, or too little knowledge of his fubject refpecting our wants in thefe cities, to propofe any effectual remedy for them.

In this general view, the fuperiority of the F. H. is apparent, inafmuch as it has preferved 1 in 3, to be 8, 9, and 10 years old, as we now fee before our eyes. The calculation of the parifh officer, as I have heard fome of them fay, *when he thinks of preferving any*, is but 1 in 5. The F. H. received by *thoufands*, the parifhes only by *hundreds*. If the F. H. were to receive by hundreds only, it is probable it might fave 2 in 5, if not 1 in 2.

4. I will not make *any* complement at the expence of my veracity, tho' I fhould have been civilly treated by the F. H. but what appears to me to be *true*, and for the fervice of my country, *that* I mean to fay, at leaft on *this* occafion. I am clear in opinion, that if the F. H. had continued to receive in fuch numbers as *four thoufand* per annum, they would not have preferved 1 in 3, nor 1 in 4, nor known how to manage the thoufands they might preferve. I do not fuppofe fo much *virtue* to be exercifed in behalf of children under any corporation government, or under a notion of their being deprived of parental connections, as will be fufficient to countervail the very origin of all government under the great Lord and Parent of mankind. The zeal and attention of a few, in a new fcheme, may operate in a pleafing manner for a while, and anfwer the purpofe of correcting fome abufes; but in the general view of parental and filial connections, we may conclude with the poet;

" God never made his works for man to mend."

5. It

5. It is very demonftrable from the cleareft facts, that the plan of an indifcriminate reception here, confounded the material diftinction of *town* and *country*, with regard to the danger of infants lives. It encouraged the exercife of arbitrary power in general through the kingdom, in the moft tender part of property, by the parifh officer enticing women to part with their children, and frequently forcing them from the breaft. Inftead of promoting the great rule of retaliation, with regard to the lawlefs commerce of the fexes ; by the great facility of throwing children into this grand refervoir, it prevented marriage, and injured the morals of both *male* and *female.*

6. It is no lefs obvious on the other hand, and ought to be equally infifted on, that this hofpital being properly reftricted, it will be productive of the greateft good. It is generally our misfortune to go into *extremes*; and this has been the cafe in regard to the F. H. From doing *too much* we do *nothing.*

7. When it is confidered, and duly examined, how unfit many of the parifhes are to be trufted with the lives of infants, and what difficulties fome find in the execution of their office, the utility of the F. H. will be apparent beyond all contradiction. There hath not yet been any fuch effectual legiflative enquiry made, as is neceffary to reform the abufes exifting. A general infpection, and a fair and judicious report of the circumftances of each parifh being made, fuch regulations may be prefcribed by authority, as the exigency requires. Some parifhes have been reformed, others which I have mentioned are now under reformation, and feveral may be eafily put on a better footing. How far the moft offending may be trufted to give a free confent, where *expence* is in queftion, and confequently to deliver a fair

and

and open detail of their paſt and preſent ſituation, I muſt leave the world to determine.

8. I can only hope the H. of C. will be pleaſed to call for all the *abſtracts* of the regiſters, if not the regiſters themſelves, ſince June 1762, to December 1765 incluſive, now in the hands of the company of pariſh clerks; and in due time order an in-ſpection to be made, that as the caſe may appear, ſuch pariſhes as uſe workhouſes and places unfit for infants to *live* in, may be obliged to recur to the F. H.

9. I alſo hope that whatever notions ſome of the gover-nors of that hoſpital have entertained of their dignity in a corporate capacity, on the principles of a F. H, or literally a-greeably to the charter for the *maintenance and education of ex-poſed and deſerted young children*, they will do themſelves the ho-nor to ſtand forth as the protectors of the real diſtreſſed in-fant, whether he is a *foundling* or not. The intention of the act for the regiſter may be improved, into the making every pariſh which is *able* to preſerve infants a true F. H. for their own diſtreſſed children : but every one that is not able to do this, ought to be obliged to have recourſe to the corporation of the F. H.

10. It is more eaſy for 147 pariſhes to take care of 60 or 80 children each, if in a courſe of years they have ſo many alive, than for an hoſpital to take care of tens of thouſands. The ſcheme ſeems to be as abſurd as the idea of *univerſal mo-narchy* formerly imputed to the extravagancy of French pre-ſumption. The common people's calling the regiſter act, *An act for keeping children alive*, is a plain indication *they* underſtand it to be of that tendency ; and conſidering that ſeveral pariſh

are

are already moved by humanity, to be attentive to the legiflative authority in the prefervation of the lives of children, others will improve on the *example*. This will appear not only on the face of the regifters, but by their giving poor women a *fhilling* or *eighteen pence*, or perchance *two fhillings* a week for a certain time, to affift them in nurfing their own children, which is by far the fafeft method in many cafes.

11. As every thing in this country depends on fafhion, it may in its turn become fafhionable for parifhes to preferve the lives of the infant poor within the bills of mortality. But it muft be thofe who are humane, and can *command money* for the purpofe.

12. If any parifh *cannot*, or more properly *will not* ufe fuch endevors to keep their children alive as reafon and experience fuggeft to be neceffary, and a greater proportion die than ought to go off the ftage of life in the common courfe of nature, fuch parifh ought furely to be obliged to apply to the F. H. and thank heaven there is fuch an inftitution. And if this were the cafe, the governors of that hofpital would know what they were about. They would adminifter a *remedy* where they were fure of a *difeafe*, and act as friends to their country and mankind, without doing any mifchief.

13. If the governors of the F. H. will enter into the fpirit of fuch a plan, they muft confider how to fubdue the difficulties that may arife. I hope they will not conjure up any upon a fufpicion of being lefs mafters of the children, for then they may eafily fruftrate the pureft and moft confiftent dictates of policy and humanity. Such a plan as this will do much better in this country than feparating parents and children for ever.

It

It will be abſurd to talk of their charter being intended for a quite different purpoſe, if that purpoſe cannot be made to anſwer. If the mode being changed, and new powers are neceſſary, let them be confidered. But a charter which doth no good, or the proper uſe of it never *rightly* underſtood, is a *pompous nothing*.

I am perfuaded the gentlemen who direct mean well, and I hope will maturely confider their meaning. It is better late than never. Something of this kind ſhould have been done ſo long ſince as 1739, when Captain *Coram* ſucceeded in obtaining the charter in queſtion. It might then have become a ſubſtantial object, and preſerved at leaſt *twenty* or *thirty thouſand lives* which have been loſt, without hurting the hair of one infant's head, who was not otherwiſe in greater danger.

14. If nothing *is* done in this way, or there ſhould not appear to be any *neceſſity* for doing any thing in it; I queſtion much if they can confiftently find any other object wherein they may be employed, without mixing a great portion of evil with the good. And if the laſt proves to be the caſe, they may be contented with the good they intended; and when they have placed out their children now on hand, refign their office. But for my own part, *I ſee not how we can give up the F. H.* call it by what other name we pleaſe, without cutting down the only prop there is to prevent ſome hundreds of children yearly being buried in the ruins of humanity by ſeveral of the pariſhes in queſtion.

15. I remember ſome of the leading members of the F. H. making light of the *regiſter* in queſtion, alledging, that pariſh-officers had no right to ſend children into the country to be nurſed, without the *conſent* of their parents; and that their parents were *perverſe* and would not conſent. As if a parent ſhould ſay, " You

M " ſhall

" *shall* take my child, but I will dictate to you how you shall
" nurse and preserve it, or how you shall *destroy* it." The fact
contradicts this notion. If the governors of the F. H. should
think it necessary to be vested with authority to retain a child,
the same powers they already possess may answer; at the worst,
the cases wherein they will be called on to do what they may
not approve, cannot be more than the parishes are now subject
to; they will probably not be so many. We must not frighten
ourselves with apprehensions of *evils*, and make our *fears* instrumental to the defeat of our own purposes: they will not
be subject to many *capricious exactions*.

16. Let what will happen, it is evident that in a country
where the poor are provided for, as with us, no distress can countenance a plan which *forcibly* tends to annihilate all parental
tenderness and authority, all filial and fraternal love. This seems
to be putting the ax to the root of free government and pure
religion. In countries where *mere foundling* hospitals prevail, it
is but a wretched traffic, imperfectly calculated to supply the
want of a *poors rate*, and to provide for the vicious indulgences
of the clergy to whom marriage is not permitted.

17. That some parents are worse than *no parents*, is indubita-
ble; and so are some members of the community, in the vulgar phrase, not worth hanging; but this authorises no one to
drag them to the gallows. The world, since the crime of *Adam*,
never was without sore parts, and numberless blemishes, nor do
I expect it ever will be; but there are some general rules by
which we must mark out the road to virtue and happiness, both
to individuals and a state; and the great land-mark from which
we must take our departure, is parental love and filial duty.

18. Upon

18. Upon the whole, some of these parishes must be *compelled* to do one of these things ; they must send their children to nurse in *a proper manner in the country* ; or take other salutary and effectual measures, which I do not comprehend, for their preservation : or they must deliver them to the F. H.

The great evil arises from the want of attention in parishioners ; and this I fear is too aptly set forth in a letter I have lately read *(a.)*

If

(*a*) Extract of a letter from *Honestus*, to the Gazetteer, the 21st March, who, after complaining of the intrigues of churchwardens to keep power in their hands, recommends to parishioners, as the only expedient, as follows ;

" 1. That the reputable house-keepers in general, of every parish, make it a point on the election day, to give an early and punctual attendance at church at the time appointed, or rather before, to converse together and look round among themselves, for a proper set of officers. Such a numerous and respectable appearance of disinterested gentlemen, will check and over-awe the junto, and prepare the way for a regular, calm, and fortunate election.

2. Mark well, which way the drunken interest points, (for they cannot hide themselves) and all unite to oppose an election which has been previously and clandestinely carried over your heads.

3. Let this opposition be general to all the officers of their proposing, that are known to herd with them. You must break the combination at once, by chusing a whole set of officers, whose hands are clean, and totally free of all connection with the cabal ; without this all will be in vain. If you could chuse two or three angels to serve along with a remnant of the old sort, they cannot serve you, they might plague themselves, but the benefit arising to the public would be very imperceptible ; and they must either run with the impure current, or be at open variance and enmity.

4. Above all things, guard against men who are known to be of arbitrary principles, who have shewn themselves eager *to dragoon parishioners into pernicious measures, by the terrors of the law, rather than consult the body of parishioners* ; the consequences of chusing *them* must be lasting and fatal.

5. Strive

If, notwithſtanding the great tenderneſs of the legiſlature, in making a law expreſsly for the purpoſe; and pointing out by a ſchedule, or form of a regiſter, what was expected to be done, they regard it ſo little, as after *three and a half* years, to make a proper proviſion in the country only for 74 in 995, under 12 months old; and of 800 ſtill in imminent danger, for a yet ſmaller proportion; what are we to expect hereafter of thoſe who are the moſt deficient?

19. It is obvious if this deſign takes place, the pariſhes ſending their children to the F. H. muſt pay for their nurſing to the time of their death, if they die, or till they are returned to *parents* or *friends*, or placed out. If there is any pariſh in theſe vaſt cities ſo miſerably poor, in a comparative view,

as

5. Strive to chuſe men of congruent principles, and liberal ways of thinking, who will glory in each others company to unite their joint efforts to ſerve the public.

6. If fortunate enough to make a delicate, judicious choice of men, whom you can confide in, apply to the gentlemen elected, to inform them, that the pariſh does not want their money, but ſtands in need of their ſervice; that it is not meant as a trap to catch fines, but to engage men of honor and ability in the ſervice of the public.

7th, and laſtly, Though I recommend a ſpirited, vigorous oppoſition to the pre-concerted meaſures of an over-bearing party, yet I would equally recommend moderation, good humour, and a calm temper, as the ſureſt means of compaſſing the deſireable end abovementioned."——He then goes on;

" As I may not, probably, have leiſure to addreſs the public on this ſubject before the critical day be over, which will determine the fate of pariſhes for the enſuing year, I will conclude with my hearty and ſincere wiſhes for ſucceſs to all honeſt intentions, and laudable endevors, that all things may be done decently and in order, and for the beſt purpoſes of promoting peace and tranquility on the moſt ſure and permanent foundation,—truth, honeſty, virtue, and public ſpirit."

as to be unable to levy a poor's rate adequate to this want, they will of courfe plead their *inability to fend the children to the* F. H. *to pay for their nurfing.* If this fhould *tempt* them to reject any diftreffed infant whom they ought to receive, or receive them *in order* that they may *die* in their hands, which I am forry to think is no extravagant fuppofition; if there are fuch parifhes, the F. H. might accept fo much the fmaller weekly allowance, and fupply the defects by their own little funds; fhewing the cafe to the world, and trufting providence, in hopes the benevolence which fuch a humane conduct would naturally call forth, would engage the attention of the pious and munificent. If this failed, collections might be made, by authority, from the richer parifhes to fupply the poorer. There are many refources which neceffity may point out. Whatever *means* reafon and experience fuggeft, the *end* ought to be purfued. In the mean while, this muft be apparent as the fun in his meridian glory; the F. H. would be no longer an object of jealoufy, difguft, or indignation, but of love, approbation and applaufe. If it did not appear as a *deity* with *præternatural* power to raife children from the grave, it would be vefted with the office of a *guardian angel,* to fnatch them out of the jaws of it.

Thus the hofpital might produce thefe children to the world, as fo many living monuments of the moft exalted policy, the tendereft humanity, and the pureft religion, whilft it fhined forth as an example to engage the *love* of every good parifh officer, and the *fear* of thofe, whofe conduct might remain in any refpect doubtful.

20. I

20. I fet forth in the title of this fection, by fuppofing children might be fent from fome parifhes, as far as *four* years of age. If they are *orphans*, and have no immediate profpect of being taken out by any friend or parent, there feems to arife as ftrong reafon againft keeping *them* in fuch workhoufes, *even at feven years old*, as do not preferve infants, as for the *infants* themfelves. If the F. H. fends fuch children to proper infpectors in the country, not approving of keeping them in towns, and places them out early, fo that their health and morals may be preferved, is it not giving a noble employment to the hofpital, and faving fubjects to the ftate? The charge in this cafe may be made lighter to the parifhes, as the time the child will be at their expence will be fhorter; and we may be fure parifh officers will not bring fuch children wantonly. This article is *fecondary* to the other of infants; but when one is digefted, it may be hoped the other will be taken under confideration, fo that no good, which *can* be done, may be omitted.

SECT.

S E C T. IX.

Some Obſervations on the Employment, Clothing, Expence, Diet, Cleanlineſs, &c. neceſſary to the welfare of the Poor, particularly young Perſons.

1. THERE cannot be a principle more ſelf-evident than this :—Where proviſion of all neceſſaries is provided, whether little or much work be done, there little work *will* be done. At the ſame time it ſhould be conſidered how to make labor as pleaſant, or to ſpeak more to the heart, as little *irkſome* as poſſible, and with a tender regard to the meaſure of a young perſon's ſtrength of body or mind.

2. A judicious tranſition from the *book* to the *loom*, the *ſpade*, the *hoe*, the *knitting-needle*, &c. may render all pleaſant, eſpecially if the book, at the ſame time that it teaches to read and inſtruct, ſupplies entertainment to the fancy.

3. An early habit of the labors of the field, eſpecially in the country, ſeems to be neceſſary. Tools for gardening being adapted to children's ſtrength, it is amazing how eaſily they acquire a facility in the uſe of them, as they do in common life, to drive a cart, or a plough, or attend cattle.

4. But as it is their fortune to depend on the labor of their own hands, wherever there is an opportunity of teaching, they ſhould learn the ſeveral duties of domeſtic life.

Whether a boy is intended for the ſea or the field, *domeſtic* ſervice, or *mechanic* arts, it is probable he will depend on his

own

own induſtry and ſkill to keep his perſon in a decent manner. Therefore what can be more uſeful to teach him, whilſt he is young, than to mend his own clothes, (ſhoes excepted) and to knit his own ſtockings, that he may have an early ſenſe of the benefits of induſtry. Being always whole and tight in his garments, and ſaving his money, he will hereafter teach his own children to follow his example. Thus acquiring a habit of cleanlineſs, and a decent reſpect for his own perſon, it will be the beſt preſervative of his comfort, and an antidote againſt that vice and profligacy which predominates amongſt common people, eſpecially when they become dirty or ragged, as experience proves.

5. With regard to females, no leſs the care of God and men, it is ſo much their peculiar province to handle the needle, that they cannot be truly uſeful to themſelves or others without it. Therefore they ſhould be taught not only to *mend,* but to *make* their own cloathing; alſo to make and mend houſhold linen, and to clean what elſe regards the kitchen and table. If any thin frock is neceſſary to wear, as a cover to their clothes, with a view to keep them clean, it ought to be provided. Such articles of oeconomical inſtruction are not generally attended to in the education of ſuch poor children, tho' their bread ſo much depends on this kind of labor; and their ideas neceſſarily enlarge in proportion as they ſee the immediate uſefulneſs of their own induſtry.

Nor need any inſtruction of this kind prevent the girls or boys *ſpinning,* or, when they are big enough, *weaving;* but this ſhould be conſidered as a *ſecondary,* not a *primary,* conſideration :

fideration: for if the children are not 'prenticed to fpinners or weavers, their knowledge will hardly be of much ufe to them.

6. I have heard it remarked by fome judicious perfons, that a child is half the ftature he ever will be of at three years of age: and I have obferved that parifh children are generally fmall. The fame has alfo appeared to me in regard to the *foundlings,* though it is fuppofed that the moft part of thefe have been *wet nurfed.* People of fmall ftature have not always the leaft ftrength or beauty; but we are naturally ambitious of being tall as well as comely. And indeed attention fhould be had to the *breed of men* in a nation, as to the breed of *horfes, fheep,* or *cows,* as much as the nature of the thing, and the liberties of the people admit. Whatever tends to promote health in the pure air of a village, is much better for the animal as well as the rational part, than the more impure air and vicious cuftoms of great cities, and large towns.

7. We perpetually complain of the dearnefs of the neceffaries of life. As riches have increafed, fo has luxury, and with this an impatience of gratifications; fo that from the landlord down to the laborer we prey on each other. However, it is not contradictory to recommend parfimony at the very moment we complain of fo many infant poor being *ftarved.* We often go into extremes: we fpend fo much even for our *adults* in parifh houfes, that fome cannot, or think they cannot fpare any thing for infants; at leaft it is fo in *many parifhes* in thefe cities, and this is the caufe of fo hideous a mortality of their infants. But it alfo arifes from the want of knowledge, and of the practice of making their money anfwer all neceffary purpofes.

N

8. With

8. With regard to an ample fupply of animal food, as the nation has grown richer, I apprehend we have confumed more. We have happily increafed the growth of corn, for *foreign* as well as *home* expence, but it may be feared we fhall have the lefs pafture land. It muft follow that we fhould have greater plenty of animal food, and enrich the ftate and individuals, and promote induftry by our gain, if whilft we acquire a fufficiency of corn for exportation, we confume fomewhat lefs bread and meat. What is great abundance in all other countries that I have feen, is great fcarcity with us. The very poor think themfelves wretched, and fo do our domeftic fervants, if they do not *fill their bellies,* as it is vulgarly called ; and they do *fill them,* and confume more folid food than they need, and confequently create a larger expence than is neceffary.

9. The remedy of this evil feems to depend much on the fimple method of preparing diet, whereby both the animal and farinaceous fubftance may go farther. It is well known that an excellent dinner may be prepared for lefs than *two-pence* each, where 15 or 20 perfons eat together, or where a part of a family is compofed of women and children. The mefs may even furnifh three or four ounces of meat, not of the moft expenfive parts of an ox, a fheep, or a hog, but what is equally good. Meat, vegetables, and roots being properly boiled together, is the only fecret by which the very water is converted into fubftantial aliment. This requires a little pepper and falt, and to be thickened with bread or oatmeal; the laft I apprehend to be the beft. But here we are alfo deficient : the oatmeal we ufe is not clean, and generally in a ftate of fermentation or putrifaction : we fhould introduce *kiln-dried clean oatmeal, fuch as*

the

the King uses for the seamen, on which there is no loss : we might then be sure of strengthening our *mess,* and rendering it no less agreeable than comfortable and nourishing. Where *firing* is wanting, there more *cheese* may be consumed ; otherwise I consider the mess above-mentioned as preferable to cheese or butter. A custom of this kind might also encourage so much gardening as is necessary to produce the vegetables and roots ; and the landlord would find his account in allowing small spots of land to his cots or houses.

10. Milk is confessedly a happy part of diet, especially for young persons ; and we enjoy a much greater abundance of it than the people who live in hotter or colder climates.

11. In general we also make our bread too white, which is another national expensive prejudice. And how shall she prepare the good dinner I have just mentioned, who lays out the two-pence in *tea* and *sugar?* Are not our very poor distressed by this extravagant expence, which has little to recommend it but that it brings in a large revenue, according to the *fancy* of the people : but surely the poor cannot in the same breath complain of *want,* if they will be so *stupidly negligent* of their own comfort and support.

12. I do not mean to abridge the poor of a reasonable quantity, but I believe they often times eat more than they need ; especially those that sit still and doze away their time. It is a vulgar notion, that a young person cannot eat too much. I believe *they* often die of repletion, and more suddenly than adults ; granting that all animals which are strong and live long, eat more in proportion to their bulk than others of the same species of more slender appetites ; yet it doth not follow but that the

N 2

strong

ftrong may be guilty of excefs. The quantity neceffary depends in a great meafure on habit, and likewife on the degree in which we toil and labor.

13. Confidering the parifh poor as the object under our immediate deliberation, particularly children, I am perfwaded we might, partly by the increafe of their induftry, without the leaft act of tyranny, or want of humanity; and partly by mere *cookery* of their diet, diminifh not increafe the expence of parifhes, and yet provide very amply for infants. With regard to their helplefs ftate, the fupport of a young child, without a mother, fhould be confidered as more expenfive than the maintenance of a grown perfon: whereas according to the ufual computation in fome *flaughter workhoufes, no expence at all is beftowed upon them.*

14. In regard to their *beveridge,* though I think tea and fugar for the confumption of the poorer part of the people is a glaring abfurdity; I am for promoting our own produce, I would encourage the ufe of good cherifhing fmall beer; I confider it as adapted to our climate, and peculiarly correfpondent with the ftate of the laboring poor. It *chears, invigorates,* and *nourifhes:* without it our lower claffes would not be half the people they are. The revenue is nourifhed by it: firft by the tax on malt, and next by the *labor* that beer produces. But when beer is too *new* or too old, young perfons or old ones had better drink good water, as the poverty of many obliges them to do.

15. As to young perfons living as much in the open air as the feafons will admit, it is the way to acquire health; but I apprehend the *head* fhould have covering, as parifh children have, be it ever fo light or fo fmall. There is alfo a medium in point

of

of drefs, which every *climate* points out to the people of the whole earth. *Ours* requires a coat and waiftcoat, which is a fecret, I fuppofe, that hath been difcovered ever fince our fore-fathers difcontinued the ufe of fkins of beafts, or the manufactory of wool was known. Let the under-garment be made of ever fo flimfy a woollen cloth, it ferves for warmth in *winter*, when a coat is *buttoned*, and coolnefs in *fummer*, when it is *opened*. Heat and cold operate equally to prevent the vigor of conftitutions. We muft confider what is comfortable to the body, or we fhall not nourifh the animal part, fo as to become tall, ftrong, or beautiful. When refinements are made againft *nature*, fhe generally fhew us a trick in the iffue.

16. What is moft wanted in all public affemblings of poor or rich, is *fweet air*. Where numbers are congregated, it is im-poffible to preferve the air pure, without the affiftance of ventilation and fometimes *not with it*.

17. It is found to be of the greateft advantage in an infirmary, to ufe a boiler with herbs, with a tin tube to communicate the fteam to the room. This medicates the air, and is of fovereign efficacy, contributing to the fpeedy recovery of patients, and the fafety of thofe that vifit them. It has been proved by fome years experience in the F. H.

18. The hanging up linen cloths dipt in vinegar, is alfo an article of great importance to correct a putrid air; and I am amazed gentlemen of the faculty do not order this fimple expedient upon all occafions, where the air is in any degree foul, as happens fo often in workhoufes, as well as the boiling of herbs, and communicating the fteam. The advantage of vinegar in wafhing decks of fhips, is found to be an admirable prefervative

under

under the moſt dangerous circumſtances; and vinegar may be made at a very cheap rate.

19. I could never hear any good reaſon aſſigned, why children of 6 or 7 years old are not *regularly* taught to comb their own hair, and waſh, not their faces and hands only, but alſo their *feet, mouths,* and *teeth,* and keep *the reſt of their body clean.* The habit of it would contribute to the comfort and prolongation of life, and greatly invigorate them. They might alſo learn much earlier than is uſual, to cut their own nails. The time allowed for ſuch duties, *when learnt,* need not be long. But it requires more inſtruction to do theſe things properly, than is conſiſtent with the ignorance and lazineſs of common nurſes. An active and intelligent matron, who is not *tyrannical,* and yet will be *obeyed,* is the ſoul of an hoſpital or a workhouſe.

20. Cleanlineſs is one of the moſt ſubſtantial advantages of riches; and why ſhould not the *poor* enjoy the common bounties of heaven, *air* and *water?* Why ſhould they not be *taught,* that the great parent of mankind is as indulgent to them as to the rich; provided they will be *induſtrious?* That if the rich are *lazy,* they will be *filthy:* if the poor are induſtrious, they will be cleanly.—It is allowed, that cleanlineſs is to the *body,* what virtue is to the *ſoul.* The poor are equally with the rich the care of one common parent; and whatever enjoyments they can attain, at ſo eaſy an expence, tending to promote their happineſs in their proper ſphere; it ſhould be taught them *early,* that they may at the ſame time learn to ſend up their hearts in gratitude to their maker, for the *comforts* they daily receive.—The moſt filthy occupations in life, require the moſt knowledge how to refreſh nature under its toils: but proper *inſtruction* and habit,

go far in all thefe refpects. In very hot, and very cold climates, the poor as well as the rich ufe baths : with us it may be done by the affiftance of a little water and coarfe linen.

21. There are but few charity fchools or workhoufes governed upon fo cleanly a plan, tho' it coft nothing but induftry to promote the health, vigor, and immediate happinefs of the objects themfelves, and the welfare of our country.

22. As to high-days of cleanlinefs for *parade*, in London, I make no objection to it. Such fights pleafe the bulk of mankind. If fome *cynical* gentlemen are difpleafed, it is becaufe the world will never be juft as they would have it. But I mean nothing of parade or fhow, delicacy or expence, but folid cheap comfort, health and happinefs, eafily obtained by authority and inftruction, and probably not to be acquired without fuch means.

23. I apprehend our common people are the moft actively laborious in the world; but they are often as carelefs of their *bodies* as of their *fouls:* would they be lefs laborious if they were more cleanly? The laboring people of fome other nations, appear more cleanly in their perfons, tighter and more free from rags than ours often are. The reafon may be, that *they*, from their infancy, are under a neceffity of taking care of themfelves; and *we* take care of the poor. We preferve many which they would lofe; but ftrictly fpeaking, we are not attentive to breed them up to a true fenfe of difcipline, as to what belongs to cleanlinefs, as an article wherein health, comfort, decency, and activity are concerned. Neither do we take pains to render them fo religious as they fhould be.

SECT.

SECT. X.

*The Advantage of placing out Children, being for laborious Employ-
ments, as early as poffible.*

1. THE fooner we begin to inftruct children, in temporal as
in moral concerns, the better.—*Train up a child in the
way he fhould go.* This leffon was given by a very wife man,
and it holds with regard to his being familiarized to the objects
whereby he is to get his bread; as it does in his obligations to
religion. The *poor* and *rich* muft make a journey through the
world, and the inftruction drawn from *real life,* and the united
force of *precept* and *example,* feems to be of more ufe than that
which is learnt from precept only, fhut up in fchools or hofpitals. But it is neceffary to make this *diftinction;* that where
young perfons are not early in fervitude, under the eye of a good
mafter, *in the world,* they had better be *dead* than in *idlenefs* or
vice.

2. This I apprehend to be the difference with regard to placing out children born to labor; that it be done as foon as they
can be placed out, (provided it be to fuch perfons as can employ
them in *a ufeful manner;*) or on the other hand, for keeping them
at fchool, in order to their having more *years* and more *inftruction.*
In the cafe propofed, they might be better provided with both
in the world, than they can be *out* of it; yet as there are but

few

few such *very good masters* as one would wish : some regard must be had to give the child as *good principles* as he can be supposed capable of.

3. Where there is nothing to be learnt at school, but a habit of industry, with reading, and the first rudiments of religion, there can be no reason for a child's remaining beyond the age of nine, ten, or at most eleven, but that few people will take the burthen of instructing him so young. If they will take him, and there is sobriety in the family where he is placed, it will signify but little his being but ten or eleven years old : and if there is not sobriety, what *security* will there be for him at twelve or thirteen ? As to forwardness and ability to be useful, this depends so much on vigilance and method of instruction, that some of the same natural capacity, are more *men* at ten, than others at twelve.

4. I am well assured, that children may get their bread from eight to ten years old, and from thence go on to earn three to eight shillings a week, very speedily ; but this depends so much on manufacturies, and the docility of a child, that no certain rule can be drawn from it.

5. With regard to agriculture, which I consider as the first object ; as it seems to be essential to the preservation of the *lives* of the parish poor infants of these cities, to be sent into the country to be nursed ; so I am persuaded, it will be a happy circumstance if they are *continued*, and placed out *there*, and as few as possible returned here. When they have acquired a vigorous constitution, and a decent care is taken to give them moral and religious principles, if their parents, or their own inclinations, bring them to town, as it now brings 5000 recruits annually, of the genuine country produce, *let them come.*

O   6. I re-

6. I reckon, that in the country, a child may be placed out at ten years of age, with more eafe, than at eleven or twelve in town, *proper affiftance* being given to people, in that *tract of life*, wherein it is intended he fhall get his bread. And, I fee no reafon why he fhould not be continued and 'prenticed out there. This being the condition of the reception in the parifh, parents would generally confent. If the parent fhould alter his mind, or his circumftances be changed, fo as to be able to take care of his own child, *independant* cf the *parifh*, nothing would be more proper, legal, and neceffary, than that the child fhould be returned to him *gratis*, at his requeft. Addrefs and caution not to comply with the temporary *caprice* of a father or mother, would be neceffary; but I am no friend to a plan of *feparation*. If children were always taught that their higheft honor and happinefs, is to affift their aged parents, when in diftrefs or old age, *fome* might *retain* the leffon.

7. If the child has no parents, or bad ones, the returning him to London, for a parifh work-houfe education, if we may judge from experience, will either kill him, or feldom prove the way to make him a good and ufeful fubject, or give him any chance of his becoming a prop to his aged parents. There is no reafon, but the want of a proper *infpection* of nurfes, why this is not as practicable and familiar as any thing of the kind, which the Foundling Hofpital is doing or has done. If there is any impediment to this plan, it arifes from the conftitution of the poor's laws, whereby the power and direction fo often changes hands; and fo little care is taken by *parifhioners*, into whofe hands it falls, fo that there is no fecurity for any right meafure being purfued, when it is begun.

8. If

8. If parishioners will exert themselves, they may prescribe such regulations as may become an invariable rule, not subject to the ignorance, caprice, or inhumanity of a man, whom they may happen to chuse as a church-warden, or overseer. Thus children sent into the country, may *be provided for there*. Persons of consideration in the neighbourhood of the nurseries, would then be found to assist the parishes as *inspectors*, in paying the nurse, and seeing justice done to the children, both in rearing them, and placing them out, the same as has been done for the *Foundlings*; with this permanent advantage, that these children would not be sent from place to place continually, and change counties to be brought into hospitals, or new nurseries, as the Foundlings have been.

9. This would be a work worthy the zeal of individuals, who are of weight by birth, fortune, or council; without which, I see not how any regulation of this kind can take effect. By this means, we should annually supply the country with 12 or 1500 children, whilst the *country* was *recruiting London*, and so far decrease the mortality.

10. As to the offices of life, for which such poor children are usually required in these cities; let these be done by young persons whose parents are living on the spot, not being the objects of parish charity. Considering what *tribes of lazy vagabonds* infest our streets, this scheme would make a provision for them: they would fill up vacant places, whilst agriculture prospered the more, for the common good of all.

11. And forasmuch as the mortality in all large *manufacturing towns*, of children under two years of age, is much greater

than

than in healthy *villages*; if it is meant to increase our numbers, *all parish poor infants* should be sent out to be nursed in villages, in cases where they are not nursed by the *mother*, and continued there, 'till they are fit to be returned with safety to work. The more advantageously they can be employed, the more valuable the life; and from the best computation, on examining *parish registers of births and deaths*, in such towns and villages, the difference is found to be 13 in 100 in favor of the latter, i. e. 26 per 100 die in the towns, and 13 per 100 only in the villages.

SECT.

SECT. XI.

The Benefit and Advantage of giving Apprentice Fees with poor Children.

1. WHEN children arrive to an age to be placed out, it is neceffary to confider the terms. I have heard it was a remark of the worthy and amiable citizen Sir *Thomas Harrifon*, that contentions between mafters and apprentices feldom came before him, as chamberlain, but in cafes where *money* had been given as an apprentice fee. What diftinctions Sir Thomas really made is the queftion, becaufe I apprehend in *all* cafes money is given. It is certain that young perfons would be fought for as apprentices, if there was no fuch thing exifting as *money*. But whilft there is fuch a thing, and the child wants a mafter, more than the mafter an apprentice, people will not eafily refign their pretenfions to fome pecuniary confideration for fuch purpofes.

2. However, the committee of the F. H. have lately urged to the H. of C. that they find by experience they can do *better* for children *without* giving money as 'prentice fees *than with it*; becaufe *it is fuppofed that by this means* nobody will afk for a child as an apprentice, who does not want one; or, in other words, no perfon is tempted to afk for a child for the fake of *money*. This feems to be an argument that proves too much. He that fells any thing for money, if I who buy am not careful, and confider what I am about, will be tempted to impofe on me

for

for the fake of the *money*. But thefe gentlemen, in the mean time, add, that the education given the foundlings is fuch as renders them preferable to all other children. This is a more fubftantial argument. The committee has accordingly, in 1765, put out 240 children of different ages, being near 6 in 100 of their number.

There is no difputing of facts; but 6 in 100 is not a fufficient number to judge by. I do not venture to affert that the event will not prove the confiftency of their plan, on the general principle they lay down; but it cannot be followed by parifhes, unlefs it become a *general rule*. If individuals give, as hitherto practifed, and the parifhes do not give, the parifh child cannot be ufhered into the world, unlefs it be alfo on the opinion of his fuperior education. In a fhort time the plea may become general: and if all are well educated, fo much the better; but this will not change the fyftem of money-loving.

3. The majority of people who take fuch children live from hand to mouth; and not to *affift them* feems to be rather a fpecies of impolicy, than folid oeconomy. If the child is well taught, and the mafter well chofen, there is more reafon for *giving money* than for *not* giving it. If fober people take children on reafonable terms, one would fuppofe the pecuniary confideration to conftitute thofe very terms. It is furely no reafon for mifbehaviour in either mafter or child that money was given, but rather the contrary: and the child comes to him in a more, not lefs, refpectable manner; fo that upon the whole I can hardly think this plan will ever become univerfal, or prove to be the beft rule.

5

4. That

4. That parish children are often put to people who take them for the sake of the 3 *l.* given, I believe is true. But the fault is not in giving the *money*, but in giving the *child* to such persons whose characters are not sufficiently known, or such as are of doubtful reputation.

5. The sum given with the children of the clergy, when they are placed out, is but 20 *l.* and they could not be placed out so properly without this fee. I believe some well-regulated parishes, which I consider in the same light as I do the F. H. give 5 to 10 *l.* whilst others place children frequently in bad hands for 3 *l.* only.

6. Where parishioners are not, by the tenure of lands, obliged to take children, 10 *l.* is often found too little to encourage a farmer to take one at a tender age.

7. If it is meant to usher a child into life at 9, 10, or 11, it is a tender age, and requires *assistance.* And where the characters of persons requiring apprentices are known, *as in the country they must be,* I should be rather led to suspect, that less good is intended to the child when nothing is *ask'd* for, than when a *reasonable* apprentice fee is demanded.

8. But the F. H. has the advantage of the parishes in respect to such of their children as are congregated in hospitals, from the impressions some people receive of external decency and order, compared to the wickedness which is often seen in our streets : and perhaps the *choice* there is captivates others. Add to this, these children being detached from all *parental* or *fraternal* connexions, render them preferable to others in the esteem of some persons. This circumstance may attach a child to a

master

master or mistress, if both parties are of good minds, and both behave properly; or become the greater evil, if either misbehave. In any case there can be no foundation for an invariable rule drawn from the F. H. be the event of the plan in question, good or evil.

9. But as the governors of the hospital have such numbers of children under their care to place out, it is more in their power to shew us an example than any other body of people whatsoever. And if they model their conduct on any good plan that *can* be followed, and from which any thing good may be learnt, they will do a more extensive service, than if it is confined to themselves only. Parishes should understand that the F. H. doth sometimes, and very properly, give 5, 6, or 7 *l.* in what is called *nurse money*, i. e. so much per week, when they meant to encourage a reputable person to take a child of 8 to 10 years old, who would not take such child without: but in general they incline to try what they can do, to shew us an example of a different nature for the service of the poor children; for it must be presumed they cannot have any other intention.

10. It is not only the parishes, the charity-schools, and the children of the clergy, and of persons in private life, but we find that in the earliest days of simplicty, when 5 *l.* was of three or four or five times its present value, in order the better to secure the obligations of masters, and to *assist* them, the children educated under that antient, permanent, and respectable institution of *Christ's Hospital*, the governors gave an *apprentice fee* of 5 *l.* and continue to give it, without doubt upon this solid principle, that it cannot from the reason of things be expected any one

taking

taking a child, or young perfon, can do fo well *without* a pecuniary aid, as *with* it. If the abufe of the thing, in *fome*
inftances, can be proved a good reafon againft the thing it-
felf, in *all* cafes, then I would vote for the total abolition
of the cuftom. But as I apprehend it will be difficult to
prove that the ceafing to give money with children, put out
as apprentices, will mend *their* manners, or the manners of their
mafters, I cannot advife any fuch meafure till I fee more of
the event.

11. The fervice to be done is the chief object in *fervitude*,
and upon this principle the child fhould be kept till the age of
12 to 15, as many are, and yet give money ; but when it is confidered that this creates a confiderable expence, and that the child
is fubject to acquire habits, and to lofe a confiderable portion of the
docile part of life : that imitation forms the capacity in the mechanic or laborious employments ; and that the fooner young
perfons are familiarifed to the objects whereby they are to
get their bread, the more expert they will be; it *follows*,
that the fooner they are placed out the better, *provided* they
can manage their own perfons with propriety, and that the
mafter has fenfe and virtue enough to treat and employ them
properly.

12. On the other hand, it is as certain that the apprenticefhips
of *fome parifh children* is as great a fcene of inhumanity, as the
fuffering others to die in infancy, as if they were not entitled to the common rights of human nature. On this
principle the caution of the governors of the F. H. is commendable ; but I rather apprehend they will, in the iffue, find

P
they

they defeat their own end, for this plain reafon, that great caution, and *a good apprentice fee, is a much better thing than great caution only.* The fault imputed to parifhes is placing out children too young, with too little attention to whom they are given, and with too little affiftance as an encouragement for proper perfons to take them.

SECT.

S E C T. XII.

The Abſurdity and Danger of placing out Children to the Age of 24,
a Part of the Statute of the 43d of Eliz. appearing neceſſary to be
reformed.

1. WHETHER the pariſhes or the F. H. give money or
not, I am ſure there is a glaring abſurdity in ad-
hering to the liberty granted by the ſtatute of the 43d Eliz.
reſpecting the placing out boys till the age of 24, as practiced by the pariſhes as well as the F. H. If under the ſanc-
tion of this law, advantage is taken of a child before he can
judge for himſelf, and to ſave a few pounds in the fee, he is
placed out in an apprenticeſhip to a taylor, a ſhoemaker, a car-
penter, a ſmith, a maſon, a peruke-maker, a baker, a butcher,
or ſuch neceſſary employments, from 10 or 12 to the age of 24, we
muſt not be ſurprized at the miſchiefs which uſually attend ſuch
apprenticeſhips. That they are a fruitful ſource of contention,
and calamity to pariſh children, and no leſs to their maſters;
many who adminiſter juſtice in theſe cities, can tell. The maſter,
aſpiring at too much ſervice, defeats his own end. He cannot
be ſerved with ſo much alacrity towards the age of 18 or 19,
when a lad knows he is to ſerve till 24, as when his ſervitude
ends at 21; nor has a young man ſo good a chance of coming
into the world with his maſter on his own account, if the maſter
may diſpoſe of him as his property till he is 24.

P 2

2. As

2. As foon as a lad finds himfelf to be 21, it is probable, if he is well inclined, and of a fober difpofition, he will think of *marriage*, and if he is not foberly inclined, he will as furely think of running away from his mafter. It is our intereft to encourage early marriage among the common people : and I fuppofe, that many of the fathers of the ftouteft men in the kingdom, were not above 21 when their fons were born ; fhall we then bind him by a legal contract, and keep him in a fervitude totally inconfiftent with the conjugal ftate, to the age of 24 ? Common apprenticefhips are for *feven* years ; the indentures of girls generally run to the age of 21, or *marriage*. Is not the *male* a *man* alfo at 21 ? If fuch a poor boy is placed out at 12, if his indenture is not extended beyond the age of 21, ftill he ferves *nine years*. This is the age of *manhood*, for the poffeffion of the largeft fortunes, in the richeft empires.

3. Let us fuppofe a lad, admonifhed by a juftice of the peace for negligence in his apprenticefhip, at the age of 21 ; if he fhould plead his own caufe, and fay, " I was too much a minor to be confulted, whether I fhould be bound till the age of 24. Tho' it was my fortune to be thrown upon a parifh, I am a *britifh fubject*, and fee no reafon, why I have not a title to the enjoyment of my freedom, at the age of 21. If the parifh officers had acted by me, as they would chufe to have been done by, they would have found a mafter for me, to ferve for 9 years inftead of 12. If they were abfurd, or cruel in the exercife of their authority, I had rather ftand to the event, with refpect to the laws of my country, than ferve my mafter any longer. I think I have done him very good and faithful fervice, and was in hopes he would have let me off at

21; if he will not let me off, I will not work for him any longer, and let him do his worſt."

4. A ſenſible ſpirited young fellow might make ſuch a ſpeech,
and yet have a very good heart. And what would any intelligent juſtice of the peace ſay? Could he *in his heart* condemn
ſuch an apprentice?—Is it not better to aboliſh an abſurd tyrannical cuſtom? To keep the poor from being licentious, they
ſhould have a reverence for laws; but if this part of the ſtatute
is productive of the breach of law, it had better be abro-
gated.

5. Suppoſe a boy put out to a *mariner* till the age of 24, be
he 10 or 12 or 13 years of age, he is ſo far conſidered as a man
at the age of 18, that in time of war the king callenges his
ſervice. Is his maſter to be paid for all the toils and bloody
conteſts this brave young ſeaman may be engaged in for the
courſe of ſix years?—So it is, in the caſes of ſuch 'prenticeſhips,
of which there are many. By the tyranny of cuſtom the
maſter is legally entitled to the *pay*, and producing his indenture, doth frequently claim it, and is paid.

6. Let us conſider, that times are altered from Q. Elizabeth's
days. Such young perſons as theſe, are not ſuppoſed to be placed out in employments of great truſt, or great ingenuity. Such
occupations may repay the ſervitude till 24—And ſuch apprenticeſhips do frequently not commence till the age of 17;
but this in queſtion is a ſpecies of ſlavery; and in every view of
it, the cuſtom ought to be aboliſhed. It will be one ſtep towards regulating the conduct of pariſh officers, or governors
of hoſpitals, in reſpect to poor children; and tend to reſtore a
free and equitable principle of œconomy in parochial adminiſtra-

tion.

tion, and the peace and good order of fociety, for if it becomes general, as to parifh children, and that no child fhall be plac-ed out beyond the age of 21, unlefs he is turned of 16 years of age, we fhall cut up the root of this practice. I do not prefume to touch the law in any other part, which I may not fo well underftand.

S E C T. XIII.

*The Neceſſity of a religious Education as the Foundation of a free
Subjection to human and divine Laws, and a Propoſal for
the Promotion of it by the moſt ſimple and practicable Expedient.*

1. THE permanent belief and mature conſideration of the
immortality of the ſoul, opens men's minds to a ſenſe of
the true genius and ſpirit of chriſtianity, and a contempt of all
things that claſh with their hopes of happineſs after death. But
men born to fortunes, or providentially acquiring them, are generally anxious for more and greater acquiſitions, and ſpend
ſo much of their time in the purſuit of them, as to forfeit
many enjoyments which are agreeable to the dignity of their
nature. Thus in the eſteem of the philoſopher and the chriſtian, the *poor* have oftentimes the advantage, tho' their poverty
expoſes men to ſuch wants as operate equally ſtrong as temptations. Thus reaſon and experience prove, that as ſurely as virtue
is our ſupreme felicity, the middle ſtation is the ſafeſt, and
therefore the *beſt*. Our ſtate in general, without diſtinction of
fortune, is ſuch that we muſt perpetually militate againſt the
evil principle which predominates in our hearts, as the only
means to prevent our returning to a ſavage ſtate of life.

2. With regard to the poor, were it not for the many cha-
rity-ſchools with which this nation abounds, and particularly

theſe

thefe great cities, there is too much reafon to believe the common people would not be bred up to *any* fenfe of religion: and as they would not teach their children what they never learnt, we might eafily fee a return of antient barbarifm. As it is, if we wait till example *afcends* from the poor to the rich, or from the child to the parent, we are not likely to fee the work accomplifhed.

3. But granting as great honor and advantage to *fchools of inftruction* as they can claim, fome other aid is wanting among us for the promotion of piety, and the obedience, fubordination, and good order which naturally refult from it. And if this is not to be expected immediately from the *labors* of the *rich*, we muft feek it by fome regulations whereby their riches without their labors, may produce the end in view.

4. Money is now become fo much the idol of mankind, and particularly in this commercial nation, that it is hardly poffible to carry any defign into execution in which it has not fome fhare. And with regard to the indigent part of mankind it muft be provided in fome fhape or other. They have no chance of wealth but from induftry; but if they can receive any emolument from induftry, even in *religion*, the end in view may be happily anfwered, efpecially if it keeps up in the hearts of children the piety they learnt at fchool, or is inftrumental in teaching them what they were deficient in.

5. Accordingly I humbly propofe to the ferious confideration of all who have young perfons under their care, efpecially of the poorer part of mankind, as follows:

I. All

I. All young perfons placed out, as apprentices, from parifh workhoufes, charity-fchools, hofpitals, or other public charities, or places of induftry, giving no money as an apprentice fee, or giving lefs than 20 *l*. to be entered in a book, according to a form to be prefcribed ; one margin whereof to be left blank to be filled up with the date of the certificate, hereafter mentioned : the faid book to be paid for by the officers, governors, mafters or directors of their charities, and the entry to be made by their refpective mafters or clerks. The page or folio wherein fuch entry is made, to be inferted in the indenture.

II. A book *in twelves* to be provided, not to exceed 150 pages, which fhall contain a choice collection of texts from the fcriptures, and fuch prayers as have been ufed by the children in their refpective fchools, hofpitals, workhoufes, or places of labor, with the addition of fome other prayers; alfo particular inftructions regarding the duty of a good apprentice to his mafter. The fame likewife to contain the form of the indentures, with blanks, to be filled up, fo that the fame be a complete copy. Another of the fame book, in the fame manner, to be prefented to the mafter or miftrefs : And the books to be alfo fold publicly at the the price of fix-pence.

III. The indenture to fet forth the fum to be given at the time ftipulated, and on the following terms : *Viz.* (fuppofe) forty-two fhillings, payable on a certificate, to be granted and figned by the rector, or curate, one churchwarden, and one overfeer ; or in want of both, either the church warden or overfeer, likewife one elder of the parifh where the 'prentice ferves; the mafter and miftrefs alfo figning the fame, and declaring that they have conftantly recommended and encouraged the apprentice in praying,

Q

morning

morning and evening, worfhipping at church on the Sabbath, and keeping up in his mind a fenfe of his duty to God.

IV. The certificate fo given to be in a printed form, with blanks to fill up the names and age of the apprentice, mafter or miftrefs, and that the apprentice did at fuch a time (the name and time being in blank, to be alfo filled up) appear before him, and in the prefence of the parties figning thereto, read half a chapter in the New Teftament, which he, the rector or curate, felected, and did repeat without book, as follows, the Lord's prayer, the Belief, the Ten Commandments, and a morning and evening prayer. Two fhillings to be paid to the rector, or his curate, who examines the party, and figns the certificate, fo that *forty fhillings* remain to the mafter or miftrefs.

V. If the apprentice is deficient, permiffion to be given to return at any time within the compafs of fixteen months; the certificate not to be given to an apprentice under fourteen, nor above fifteen and a half years of age.

VI. The rector or curate to keep a fair regifter-book, in a form prefcribed, of all 'prentices who have appeared before him, and a column for the date of the certificate to be filled up, when he paffes the fame.

VII. If the certificate is not paffed at the firft appearance of the apprentice, the rector, or his curate, is to recommend in the ftrongeft terms, to the mafter or miftrefs, the confideration of the difgrace of lofing the premium, as the apprentice's name will ftand a blank in his regifter book; befides the great injury done to the apprentice, and to themfelves, by their not being more attentive in their duty to God.

VIII.

VIII. The rector or curate to be defired to read publicly, on Chriftmas-day, the names of all the mafters and 'prentices, to whom he hath given fuch certificates during the courfe of the year, that the congregation prefent, may be at once reminded of the premium, fo far as any of them may be concerned, and like-wife of the duty which they owe to God.

6. Upon this I have to obferve, that nothing can be more fimple than a propofition of this fort, as one expedient to bring the common people to a fenfe of their duty to their maker, at leaft to the knowledge of the great *out-lines* of religion.

7. Whatever hofpitals or charities may be inclined to do by virtue of their own authority, the plan might be reduced to com-mon practice; perhaps without conftituting any part of an act of parliament. If the indentures were in the firft inftance re-giftered by the rector, he would fee if the premium is demand-ed, and how the apprentice behaves.

8. In any cafe it muft be apparent, that a folemn invitation to perform the tafk required, is an object of the utmoft impor-tance, towards affifting the laboring poor to learn what belongs to their prefent and everlafting happinefs, by the ftrongeft proof that can be expected, that he who fears God, gives the beft affurance of confulting the welfare of his mafter, and the peace and happinefs of his country. And it muft be no lefs evi-dent, that fuch a pecuniary emolument, will be the beft incentive, and moft conftant monitor to good actions, whether the duty be always performed exactly as it fhould be or not.

9. As to the execution, it is not to be prefumed the rector, or his curate, will be rigid in the examination: or, on the other

Q 2

hand,

hand, fo remifs in his duty, as to render it of no effect. And as fo many muft join in the fraud, the fuppofition that this will happen, ftrikes at the foundation of all good faith, infomuch, that it implies a total indifference on the part of the mafter, as to fhewing any regard to what his 'prentice has learnt, or will learn of religious duties under him. But with a fmall portion of attention, the profit and honor, and real duty, on one fide; and the fhame, lofs, and difgrace, on the other, cannot fail of producing fome happy effects.

10. To facilitate this matter, I fay nothing of the catechifm, be it taught or not; I mean only *that* which a young perfon may really and truly underftand, and by habit he be kept in fome awe by his *belief* and *truft* in God. The gratuity will be a means of keeping the apprentice in remembrance of what hath been taught him, before he was put out, and alfo what he has learnt of his mafter, whilft it is a means of his former friends and patrons holding a connection with him.

11. In anfwer to the objections that may arife, I afk, if children, placed out as they now are, fhould be adepts in their prayers, and able to do all, or more than I have mentioned, when they went out; how is it that we know they are kept to any fenfe of their duty?

12. Such a plan as this will create the moft fincere veneration for any inftitution, which may practife it, with all people, who have any fenfe of religion. And if obedience to government depends on *religion* as well as the *gallows :* if early inftruction is the foundation of religion, and fuch inftruction may be eafily loft by neglect; the force of this propofition will be

clear

clear and apparent. I fuppofe fuch an example may lay a foundation, on which the moft regular and harmonious ftructure
of religion may be erected in *private* life, as well as in *public
charities*; and that from its nature and tendency, it cannot fail
of making fuch an impreffion on the poor, as muft produce
many good effects, in regard to their behaviour towards the great
author of nature, their *God* and their *Redeemer*.

13. To fuppofe that thefe certificates *will not be true*, is bear-
ing hard on churchmen, and the characters of the graveft parifhioners; and if a falfhood can be detected as eafily as hear-
ing a child repeat, what the certificate attefts, it will furely
argue more caprice, than good fenfe or piety, to object to the
propofition on any fuch injurious prefumption.

14. I therefore ferioufly recommend this plan, till a better is
contrived. Life doth not afford fo many opportunities of doing good, as to neglect a defign of fuch importance. I hope
thofe that mean to act *as parents* to poor children, and to do
the beft they can, to keep them unfpotted from the world, will
follow this plan, or chalk out a better.

15. It cannot be imagined, that parifh officers, or governors
of charities, can vifit children, when difperfed over a kingdom.
Alas! how few know where half a dozen fuch children are
placed out, except when they look into their books. But in this
way, *they* will be kept in mind for a few years, as if it were their
own children in queftion. And whether as parifhes, or as public
charitable inftitutions, they take cognizance of fuch certificates,
they certainly will not pay the money in queftion, but upon the
conditions ftipulated.

4

16. I

16. I apprehend, the common people will never lofe fight of *money*, though they often lofe fight of heaven. If the young perfon be 14 to 16, and fo qualified as related, and the mafter or miftrefs make a declaration, as part of the certificate, that the child has, to the beft of their belief or knowledge, conftantly faid both morning and evening prayer, fuch as fhall be repeated to the clergyman, on occafion of his giving the certificate; it can hardly fail of operating happily, not on the child only, but alfo on the mafter and miftrefs themfelves.

17. What I am urging arifes from experience; I have had frequent opportunities of knowing, from my own fenfes, that *thoufands* of the poor are in fuch grofs ignorance of religion, that they cannot even repeat the *Lord's Prayer* or the *Belief*. And I have hardly found any, though in reputable bufineffes, who offer a fingle word to their maker, when they rife in the *morning*, whatever they pretend to do at *night*.

18. Can it be thought, that children will be good or bad, but as their mafters or miftreffes keep them up to a fenfe of religious duties? Very few of the laboring part of thefe kingdoms, are bred in hofpitals. And how, as I have faid, do we know that hofpital or charity children are taken care of in this article?

19. When a child is placed out by the F. H, a parchment of inftructions, and a bible, are given: every one muft approve of this; but if a little book were compiled, containing about the fortieth part of the Old and New Teftament, and a few prayers out of the Liturgy, the Lord's Prayer, the Belief, the Ten Commandments, and a well digefted morning and evening prayer, all calculated for the purpofe of promoting moral duties, induftry, and truft in God through the Redeemer of mankind;

kind; fuch a book might anfwer the purpofe intended, in their youthful ftate, better than the *whole* of the Old and New teftament.

20. Improvements founded in reafon and the common fenfe of mankind, demand attention. Children often read the *fcriptures* with about as much underftanding of them, as a parrot could have, and as a tafk which is extremely irkfome, infomuch that many never look into the book after they leave fchool. Is it not a melancholy confideration, when religion is not even treated fo refpectfully as a political device? As children grow up, the whole of the Old and New Teftament may be recommended to them; and they fhould be affifted to relifh it. This I apprehend may be eafily done in the little book I allude to, by fkilfully pointing out what paffages are the moft effential for them to underftand and practife.

21. Thus whilft the *young* perfon is learning the way to heaven, the *elder* will find the road, which I am perfuaded they now often miftake. The knowledge and practice of their duty may ceafe to appear as a laborious tafk. Religion is feldom introduced to them clothed in her native beauty and fimplicity.

22. If any warm-brain'd enthufiaft, or capricious caviller, fhould fay, ' This is *bribing people* to be religious;' my anfwer is, It is very happy if they become religioufly inclined by fuch a bribe. The rule could not be obferved without fome true fenfe of religion; and if temporary advantages precede the temporal or eternal reward, it is but an ordinary effect of virtue, and agreeable to *his* decrees, who made the human heart.

We do not ufually fall foul of the 'Squire for the beef and pudding which he gives on Sundays to his tenants who attend

2   divine

divine fervice, fhutting out thofe who do not attend it. His intention is good; it is to give them a habit of religious duties. Surely fuch a bribe as this would promote, not injure, the reputation either of the parent, the parifh officer or governor who 'prenticed out the child; or the clergyman, the parifh-officer, the elder, or mafter, who were witneffes to the difcharge of the religious obligation mentioned in the certificate. As to the objection of the leffon being learnt *only for the occafion*, the fame argument will hold againft giving any inftruction at any time. If it is learnt, it is fo far happy.

23. This defign will be of the nature of catechifing a lad, or grown girl, in the fhorteft, moft fimple, and familiar manner. It will be a wholefome difcipline to mafter or miftrefs, and the minifter's reading the lift to whom certificates have been given fince the laft publication, will make a happy impreffion on all his congregation.

24. This plan being an additional labor to the clergy, they will be intitled to the *two fhillings* for each certificate; and thus it will be *their* intereft alfo to give fuch certificates, but furely not their *intereft* to give *falfe ones*. I dare fay fome of them will joyfully prefent the tax to the boy or girl that is well taught; and others, from their fituation, will have a very good title to receive it.

SECT.

S E C T. XIV.

The Importance of cultivating a Senfe of Religion among the Poor, and particularly in the great Duty of Prayer.

1. WE complain of this age being diffolute and thoughtlefs, and there has been too much reafon to complain in all ages. *Confideration* may be taught, as well as any thing elfe ; but it doth not appear to be in fafhion with the children of the *rich*, much lefs do the *poor* learn it. When thefe are inftructed to read, they alfo learn to repeat certain words, which are called *prayers*, and when they repeat thefe words, they call it *faying their prayers*. But if their teacher doth not queftion and inftruct them, and repeat to them, in a manner as if himfelf underftood the meaning of the words, and as if he felt the force of them, and was fenfible of the majefty of him to whom they are addreffed, with a fenfe of *his own* unworthinefs, how is the young perfon to learn any thing of this kind ? Is *he* to become a *man* before his *mafter*, or before *he* has adequate ideas of the moft fimple words, for no other reafon, than becaufe they are *intended* to be addreffed to his maker ? Doth not much of our irreligion arife from the ignorance or indolence of parents or teachers among the *poor* ? Are fuch teachers examined as to their ability, and manner of teaching ? And where is our fenfe, our wifdom, our piety, when the event is left to chance, without a

R

check

check or examination,—except when we are admitted to *degrees* in learned profeffions.

2. From the nature of our condition as men, nothing can open our minds more to a fenfe of virtue, and a proper eftimation of a tranfitory world, than the thought of *death*, and its concomitants, judgment, heaven, or hell. But as if we imagined the young perfon would grow melancholy, if we applied it clofely to his mind ; we pafs this matter over in as tranfient a manner, as if he really had very little or no intereft in it. How few fupport fuch dignity in life as arifes from a due fenfe of our condition. The *rich* refine away the moft folemn confiderations, and the *poor* treat them with indifference. We crowd to a *rarefhow*, but who attends or fends young perfons to attend the *end of this world*, and the commencement of eternity. We have an admirable prayer when we commit *duft to duft*; but I queftion if *one* young perfon, in *five hundred*, knows there is fuch a thing. Why fhould not *they* be taught *what life is?* With a little change of words it may be adapted to common ufe *(a)*, and rendered as *familiar* as it is important.

(a) ALMIGHTY God, and parent of mankind, I befeech thee of thy infinite mercy and goodnefs, to teach me to confider, that man who is born of a woman hath but a fhort time to live ; that he cometh up and is cut down like a flower ; that he fleeth as it were a fhadow, never continuing in one ftay. Teach me, O Father of mercy, to confider, that in the midft of life I am in death ; and of whom can I feek for fuccour, but of thee, O Lord, tho' for my fins thou art juftly difpleafed.—Yet, O God moft holy, O Lord moft mighty, O holy and merciful Saviour, deliver me not into the bitter pains of eternal death.— Thou knoweft, Lord, the fecrets of my heart ; fhut not thy merciful ears to my prayers ; nor thou, O bleffed Redeemer, and judge of quick and dead, fuffer me

not

important. Would a young perſon, with the natural frame of mind, which the indulgent author of nature hath given us, grow *melancholy* with the thought, that he might die at *thirteen*, when he ſees his maſter alive at *three-ſcore?* Would he not rather learn to poſſeſs his ſoul in peace, from the conſideration, that if he ſhould die he ſhall be happy.

3. I lay it down as a principle, both in morals and politics, that nothing is ſo eſſential to the life of man, as commerce with his maker. In theory, this is never denied; but in practice, it is amazing to conſider, how few learn to addreſs him with awe, and propriety of expreſſion. The *rich* are not taught it at any public ſchool; they are not taught *any reliſh* of devotion, but rather by an injudicious intruſion of too much external piety, and attendance at church, we make young lords and gentlemen ſick of devotion before they leave ſchool. *When* it is that they are reſtored to a vigorous ſenſe of this duty, the great ſearcher of hearts can beſt tell.

4. The preſent buſineſs is to take the *poor* under our patronage. So far as any ſuggeſtion of this kind may avail, I would conſider, not only the means of teaching them in the firſt inſtance, but how they may retain their inſtruction in life in the moſt effectual manner. I conſider *acquaintance with God,* as no viſionary expreſſion, but ſo far as *adoration, gratitude,* and *obedience,* differ from *careleſſneſs, ingratitude,* and *diſobedience,* we are all deeply intereſted firſt to learn, and then to teach the poor

what

not at my laſt hour, for any pains of death, to *fall from thee.* Teach me, O God, in all conditions and extremities, to rejoice in the comfort of thy holy word, and to do my duty whilſt I live, in ſteady hope of a reſurrection to immortal happineſs, through the merits and mediation of the ſame Jeſus Chriſt, the bleſſed Saviour of the world. R 2

what belongs to their peace, before it is hid from their eyes for ever.

5. I can by no means think their prayers fhould be tedious, but fhort, plain, and fimple. Some forms which are adopted, are too diffufe, too figurative in expreffion, or involved in fenfe, and upon the whole, very unfit for a child.—It is no eafy tafk to adapt prayers to the, capacity of children, and yet give them force of expreffion, tendernefs of fentiment, as addreffes to the *Father* of mankind, dignity and awe, as to the *maker* of heaven and earth.

6. The foundlings a few years fince, had a prayer of the kind I have related, full of good fenfe and piety, but in general the children could not learn it. What they now ufe (*b*) is extremely familiar to them.

7. The

(*b*) *A* MORNING PRAYER *ufed by the Children of the Foundling-Hofpital.*

O Lord God Almighty, who haft made me, and all the world, I humbly thank thee for thy care of me in the night paft. Continue thy favor and compaffion to me: keep me this day from all harm, and help my endevors to behave myfelf humbly, foberly, and godly, that I may always pleafe thee in thought, word, and deed.

O merciful Father, make me to remember, that it is by thy gracious providence I am clothed and fed, and my life preferved. Teach me to be always contented, and pray for thofe who have acted as parents to me. Give me an awful reverence of thy majefty; and make me tremble and afraid of offending thee, by any falfhood, fraud, or uncleannefs; any unjuft or uncharitable action; that I may be happy in the enjoyment of a good confcience; and never fall into that dreadful and everlafting punifhment, which waits on impenitent finners.

This I beg, O Lord, in the name of my bleffed Saviour and Redeemer Jefus Chrift. *Amen.*

7. The prayers at Chrift's Hofpital are fuppofed to be for elder children than the *foundlings*, and the moft part of their compofitions feem to be extremely good, (*c*) but not equal in dignity and fimplicity to fome prayers in the Liturgy. It is a queftion, if the requeft, that *The day-fpring from on high may now and ever fhine upon them*, though a bold and beautiful figure, is really intelligible to a child, notwithftanding the pious author might imagine it to be fo fcriptural and devout, that it muft needs be proper; but if upon examination it is not found to be proper, why fhould children ufe fuch expreffions in their addreffes to their God and Father?

8. Let

(*c*) MORNING PRAYERS *at Chrift's Hofpital.*

O God of mercy, and Father of all comfort, who of thy merciful goodnefs haft brought us to the beginning of this day: we thine unworthy children beg that the day-fpring from on high may now and ever vifit and fhine upon us: and that pardoning our offences, and continuing to be good unto us, thou wouldeft difpofe us to a better conformity to thy laws, and obedience to thy commandments, through Jefus Chrift, our Lord and only Redeemer. *Amen.*

REMEMBER not, Lord, the fins of our youth, nor the follies of our childhood: but confider whereof we are made, and from what we are fallen by the tranfgreffion of our firft parents, and be merciful unto us. O teach us betimes to number our days, that we may apply our hearts early unto wifdom, for Jefus Chrift his fake. *Amen.*

LET thy bleffings, O Lord, defcend abundantly upon the perfons and families of all our benefactors, accept their offerings, and be thou their exceeding great reward. Blefs our governors, and forget not their labour of love, which they have undergone for thy name's fake: neither fuffer thou us to be ungrateful to thee or them. We likewife beg of thee to preferve us in perpetual fafety, for the fake of our only Saviour, in whofe name and words we continue to pray—*Our Father,* &c.

8. Let us fee how the morning prayer in the Liturgy ftands as we find it, or if adapted to private ufe, with the change of a few words (d).

Here I muft obferve, that prayers which may with propriety be ufed through life, are fo far the beft to learn in childhood, if, as I fear, (though it is a bold thought) the bulk of mankind do not often learn any form of words after they grow up, except thofe of the Liturgy; and very few are qualified to pray without form, with an intenfe devotion.

9. The primitive Chriftians ufed to pray at *noon*, as well as in the morning, and at night. The Mahommedans pray at noon; and fo do the pious Jews. And I have obferved fome of the papifts in Portugal do the fame. I fee there is an excellent prayer at *Chrift's Hofpital* for *noon* (e), to which there can be no objection, unlefs it be that the idea of the fun in his meridian altitude, is introduced in a manner a child may not comprehend. The Foundlings have one to be ufed night or morning

(d) O God, my Father, and Lord of heaven, who haft fafely brought me to the beginning of this day; defend me in the fame with thy almighty power, and grant that I fall not into any fin, neither run into any kind of danger, but that all my thoughts and actions may be ordered by thy governance, that I may do all things acceptable in thy fight. This I beg, O merciful and tender Father, for the fake of Jefus Chrift, our Redeemer. *Amen.*

(e) O Father of light, fhine upon us with the fulnefs of thy grace. Do away our offences, cloath us with humility, and fill us with thy holy fpirit, that we may be enabled to do fuch good works, as thou haft ordained us to walk in: look down in compaffion upon thy poor children. Protect our tender age from the violence of temptation; ftrengthen us by thy almighty power; and as we grow in years, fo make us grow in grace, through Chrift our Lord. *Amen.*

morning (*f*), and which may ferve for noon. But as the world goes, it is well if children pray properly *twice* in the day.

10. For the evening, the children of Chrift's Hofpital have a prayer, (*g*) which, if it were to pafs through an examination, might be made to deal lefs in *figures*, and to fupplicate mercy, rather than to confefs fins, of which the children may not have been guilty, or if they have, they have very little fenfe of them: and if this is the opinion of thofe that govern, one would wifh to fee reafon prevail in all things. This however is in its favor as it ftands, that it may ferve the better when they grow up to manhood, with a fmall change of expreffion.

Thofe

(*f*) O Merciful Lord and tender Father, I moft humbly befeech thee to give me thy affiftance, that I may conftantly ftudy, and earneftly endevor to ferve thee in all things with a fincere and willing mind.

Grant that I may be moft truly thankful and dutiful to my benefactors, mafters, and teachers; harmlefs and kind to all others; that by thy grace I may always govern myfelf with patience and meeknefs, as taught by my bleffed Redeemer in his holy gofpel.—And when I die, O let me enjoy that happinefs in the life to come, which thou haft promifed to thofe who are good, and ferve thee with a true heart.

This I beg, O merciful Father, for the fake of thy beloved Son, my Saviour Jefus Chrift, who hath commanded me, when I pray, to fay, *Our Father*, &c.

(*g*) O Father of mercies, look upon us of thy great goodnefs. We have finned againft thee, and are no more worthy to be called thy children. The wantonnefs and folly of our youth prevailed upon us, the frailty and ftubbornnefs of our depraved nature have made us to err: O forgive us our fins. We come to thee heavy laden with the weight of this day's tranfgreffions: refrefh our drooping fpirits; and grant us thy grace fo to walk before thee for the future, that we may bring fruit meet for repentance, through Jefus Chrift our Lord. *Amen.*

Thofe for the Royal Family and their founders (*h*), muft be approved, though they alfo begin with a *figure*.

11. The evening prayer of the Foundlings (*i*), feems to contain a fummary of chriftianity, in theory and practice, as far as a child's addrefs to heaven can be fuppofed to extend. The prayer (*k*) faid

(*h*) WATER, we befeech thee, with the heavenly dew of thy bleffing, Chrift's holy church, particularly this portion of it in which we live: Guide, ftrengthen, and protect it. Blefs our moft gracious Sovereign Lord King GEORGE, and all the Royal Family, and all that are in authority under him. Blefs this city, and every member of it, particularly this Royal Foundation, with all that ferve in it, or do good unto it. And this we beg for Chrift his fake. *Amen.*

We praife thee for our Founders and Benefactors, and for the comfort thou haft afforded us by their means, both to foul and body: blefs, and greatly increafe their fubftance who have fatisfied the poor with bread; let their families be profperous upon earth, and a fure and full reward be given them of the Lord at the refurrection of the juft. Grant that we, with thankful hearts for all thy mercies, may chearfully do thy will, through Jefus Chrift, who liveth and reigneth with thee, and the Holy Ghoft, world without end. *Amen.*

(*i*) O God, my Almighty Creator and Preferver, accept my humbleft thanks for thy protection, and all the bleffings I have received this day paft. Forgive all the fins which I have committed againft thee this day, and make me afraid and afhamed to do any thing that is wrong. Let me conftantly remember, that thou art prefent every where, both day and night, and that all my thoughts, all my words, and actions, are open to thy view.

I now lie down to reft, O merciful and tender Father, in humble confidence that thy goodnefs will keep me in fafety; that I may arife refrefhed with fleep, in health, and ftrength, of body and mind; and when this prefent life is ended in death, O Lord, receive my foul into that happy ftate, which thou haft prepared for thy obedient children.

This I beg, through Jefus Chrift my Redeemer, who died upon the crofs, that through my obedience to thy laws, I may be redeemed from my fins. *Amen.*

Our Father, &c.

4

(*k*), said by the children in Chrift's Hofpital, in the feveral wards at night, going to bed, is highly commendable, and of fuperior dignity; it may ferve the children, when grown up to manhood.

12. But I cannot bring myfelf to think, that the prayer (*l*), is proper to be in ufe, unlefs the expreffions of *dreams and affrighting and diftracting fancies, and the horrors of darknefs,* are a little changed. The ideas of the words, create the very evils they are intended to prevent. If the children go to bed in health, with moderate diet, and trufting in their God, why all this terror? The conclufive part (*m*), is excellent.

As to the manner in which children in general are *taught,* or rather *permitted* to read prayers, or to pray, it is of all things in the world the moft *abfurd.* The fame may be faid of their
fcreaming

(*k*) LORD, let the reft we are going to, mind us of the hour of death: and now that we are going to lie down, let us confider, that it may be, we fhall rife up no more. We do earneftly, therefore, repent us of our fins, and are heartily forry for our mifdoings; and we befeech thee, give us grace fo to be fenfible of all our errors for the time to come, that the remembrance of them, may be a warning to us, to continue ftedfaft in our obedience, and ever to walk in newnefs of life, to the glory of thy holy Name, through Chrift our Lord. *Amen.*

All honor and praife be given to thee, O Lord God Almighty, for the life thou haft raifed us to by thy free grace, and for the hopes of glory: for the free courfe of thy gofpel among us, and for the minifters of thy holy word and facraments. Give us grace, we pray thee, fo to apply thefe means which thou haft afforded us, that they may become falvation to us, through ˙our bleffed Redeemer Jefus Chrift. *Amen.*

(*l*) Preferve us, O merciful God, from all evil dreams, from all affrighting and diftracting fancies, from the horror of the night, and the works of darknefs.
(*m*) Give us quiet and compofed thoughts, and fuch reft in thee, that we may fleep under the covering of thy wings, and awake in thy favor, through him who liveth and reigneth with thee and the Holy Ghoft, world without end. *Amen.*

S

screaming when they mean to *sing* with solemn devotion, and true measure. They are both a mere burlesque. I am sure a very little pains, and patience, might remedy these abuses. The absurdity of being thus trifling in religious duties, admits of no excuse.

14. As for the grace before meat, at Christ's Hospital (*n*), I make no objection, yet I wish in general to remind the world of the duty of charity as in the form (*o*). I have no objection to the grace after meat (*p*).

15. I give my thoughts with freedom, with a view to inspire a *warm* but *rational* attention to the poor in every state and condition; and I consider Christ's Hospital, and the F. II. as patterns, being conducted, each in its way, with more propriety than workhouses, or most other places of assembling the poor.

16. If a collection were made of all the forms, regulations, and domestic oeconomy, of our numerous charities in the kingdom, every one would extract the sweets of such a labor. It seems to be a work worthy of any man of sense, piety, and leisure, whether he be a deep theologist or not.

S E C T.

(*n*) GIVE us thankful hearts, O Lord God, for the table which thou hast spread for us. Bless thy good creatures to our use, and us to thy service, for Jesus Christ his sake. *Amen.*

(*o*) O GOD, our Father, we beseech thee, to supply the wants of all our fellow creatures, and inspire our hearts with gratitude and love for this and all thy mercies to us, for Jesus Christ his sake. *Amen.*

(*p*) BLessed Lord, we yield thee hearty praise and thanksgiving for our Founders and Benefactors, by whose charitable benevolence thou hast refreshed our bodies at this time. So season and refresh our souls with thy heavenly Spirit, that we may live to thy honor and glory. Protect thy church, the King, and all the Royal Family. And preserve us in peace and truth, through Christ our Saviour. *Amen.*

SECT. XV.

*Further Reasons in support of the Proposal for a pecuniary Gratu-
ity, after a certain time, to those who do their duty to poor
Children, as Apprentices, on the religious and prudential Plan
proposed.*

1. WE Protestants have no faith in the mere *Opus operatum*
but I have constantly observed, from the moment a
boy becomes profligate, or a girl a harlot, they bid adieu to their
prayers. As on the other hand, when they practice this duty, and
attend to it, in any tolerable degree, they are in a great measure
kept in awe of that *power* to whom they address their prayers.

2. I have been also several times a witness to the effect of
prayer among young persons, who have been 'prenticed out.
A little wholesome serious advice on this principle, to the master or mistress, as well as the child, pointing out what words
they should use, and upon what occasions of trespasses, and
temptations to obstinacy and perverseness, is of great moment.
A refractory boy or girl hath been thus subdued: it hath produced all the happy consequences which a belief or confidence
in the promises or protection of heaven, or the fear of punish-
ment after death, can be supposed to create in the mind of a
child, not become impenetrable to such impressions. Without talking the language of enthusiasm, can there be any
thing of so much consequence to the *poor,* as well as the *rich,* as
the custom and habit of prayer?

S 2

3. In

3. In the prefent fituation of the diffolutenefs of the *higher* ranks, as well as of the *lower*, I do not difcover how the lower can be called back, and put in a right train, fo effectually as by beginning with young perfons, not only in fchools or hofpitals, but where they are actually put into the world, and in the path wherein they are to be trained up. But how is this to be accomplifhed by any means, exclufive of the piety of the mafter and miftrefs? If they happen to be rationally *pious*, or not very *impious*, by keeping them in mind of their duty, by a *peculiar provifion* for it, we fhall at once fhame them if they neglect it, and do them honor, and give them profit too, if they obferve it. I have revolved this much in my thoughts : I have examined it at the bar of my reafon : I have compared it with long experience : I have confulted judicious difcerning verfons. In every fhape I find it ftand the *teft*.

4. To corroborate the opinion by *facts*, it is neceffary alfo to mention that whilft I was happily engaged in the fervice of the poor, during the late war, I obferved that of fome hundreds of young North Britons, who came to us directly from Scotland, none of them were given to fwearing; every one could read, and fay his prayers; and none of them were in rags.——— Among the Englifh boys, picked up in the fame manner, for the fame purpofe, forry I am to fay it, the moft part of them were in the moft filthy ragged condition, and hardly with any notions of religion.

5. Upon enquiry how it came about, that my own country boys were outdone in this way, I found the Scotch clergy had examined them yearly, and kept them to their duty. Now it is upon this very principle of experience among the dregs of mankind,

kind, and the reafon of things, I found my belief, that much good may arife from an obvious and fimple plan, whereby it will become the duty and intereft of mafter and 'prentice, clergyman, parent and child, exprefly ftipulated for in indentures, for a certain fmall fum of money, to be paid at a certain time, for the purpofe related, that our brave, induftrious, comely *Englifh boys* and *girls* may maintain what they have learnt before they were placed out, or acquire inftruction after it. It is fo evident from the reafon and nature of things, that it may be accomplifhed by fuch means as propofed, I hope parochial officers, governors of charity-houfes, hofpitals, and parents in general, will try the experiment. It is but regulating a part of the money ufually given, in a *new mode*; or giving fo much more, exprefly for a purpofe of fuch vaft importance. If it doth not produce *all* the good we wifh, it cannot fail of an ample portion.

5. As the cafe ftands at prefent, what I infift on, is, to know what clue there is, whereby to trace out, that a child is kept to his duty, a day after he is 'prenticed out. Will the mafter declare himfelf negligent? Will the child make a formal complaint to his governors or parents, " my mafter is indifferent, whether " I fay my prayers or not." As well may we expect him to complain, that he is fuffered to *play* when he fhould *work*.

6. If gentlemen who have the care of the poor, will take that for granted, which experience fo often contradicts, they cannot, at the fame time, pretend to be warm friends to the poor. And it will be abfurd to complain of the irreligion of the common people, and the fad effects of impiety, and yet ufe no rational precautions to bring them into a due fenfe of their everlafting obligations.—The way to preferve the bodies and fouls of all the poor, in public and private, is by one and the fame rule.

7. I have only to add, that although fuch a defign as this feems to be moft valuable for *thefe and other great cities and towns,* and where there are not parents and friends to admonifh young perfons or their mafters, or where their parents only corrupt them: at the fame time, if it be *true* that a very great part of our common people are ignorant and profligate, it muft be deemed a very juft and right meafure to have a *check* on them, with which it becomes their *intereft* to comply.

8. Another method indeed of providing for the parifh poor, both body and foul, is to let them *all die in infancy,* after a medium of life of *twenty-four days and eight hours,* as laft year happened to 64 in 78, in the united parifhes of St. Andrew's above Bars and St. George the Martyr: but this evil, I am perfuaded, we fhall foon fee rectified, and that all fuch prefcriptions will be condemned hereafter by the whole college of political and theological, as well as medical doctors.

S E C T.

S E C T. XVI.

A Lift of the Parifhes whofe Numbers of Children are worthy of Notice; with a curious Anecdote relating to a Parifh-Nurfe; and the Conclufion, inviting to the Exercife of Humanity to the Children of the Poor under the Care of Parifhes.

GENERAL SURVEY of the REGISTERS of the PARISHES having any confiderable Number of CHILDREN.

Thofe parifhes marked *, have no workhoufe. Parifhes without the Walls.	Born and received.	Difcharged.	Remaining.	Of whom from 1 to 4 years old.	Of whom dead.	Under 12 months old.	Of whom dead.	Dead per Ct. from 1 to 4 years old.	Dead per cent. under 12 months old.	Pages of remarks in this book.
St. Andrew, Holborn	58	13	45	22	8	23	15	35	69	
St. Bartholomew the Great	3		3							
St. Bride *	10	2	8	6		2	1		50	35
St. Botolph, Alderfgate	11		11	6	1	5	3	16	60	
St. Botolph, Aldgate	28	6	22	12	3	10	8	25	80	35
St. Botolph, Bifhopfgate	29	9	20	10	3	10	8	30	80	35
St. Dunftan, Weft	5		5	1		4				
St. George, Southwark	24	12	12	3	2	9	5	66	55	
St. Giles, Cripplegate	39	22	17	9	5	8	6	55	75	
St. John, Southwark	28	12	16	8	3	8	6	37	75	
St. Olave, Southwark	25	12	13	9	2	4	4	22	100	
St. Saviour, Southwark	48	12	36	19	10	17	8	5	48	
St. Sepulchre, Newgate	49	13	36	17	11	19	15	64	79	
Parifhes in Midd. and Surry.										
St. Ann, Middlefex	12	1	11	6		5	2		40	
Chrift Church, Southwark	16	5	11	10	5	1	1	50	100	

Parishes in Midd. and Surry continued.	Born and received.	Discharged.	Remaining.	Of whom from 1 to 4 years old.	Of whom dead.	Under 12 months old.	Of whom dead.	Dead per Ct. from 1 to 4 years old.	Dead per cent. under 12 months old.	Pages of remarks in this book.
Chrift Church, Middlefex	34	17	17	3	2	14	7	66	50	
St. Dunftan, Stepney	16	4	12	8	1	4	1	12	25	
St. George, Middlefex	19	1	18	12	8	6	4	66	66	41
St. Andrew above Bars and St. George Martyr, fometimes called St. George Queen's Square, and Holborn above Bars	141	17	124	34	20	90	64	60	71	35,57
St. Geo. Bloomfbury and St. Giles in the Fields	178	62	116	67	22	49	39	33	80	45
St. James and St. John, Clerkenwell	78	33	45	31	14	14	11	46	80	
St. John, Hackney	19	9	10	8	1	2	1	12	50	
St. John, Wapping	35	8	27	20	2	7	3	10	43	
St. Catherine, Tower	4	2	2			2	1		50	
St. Leonard, Shoreditch	65	7	58	36	8	22	6	22	27	
St. Luke, Middlefex	41	2	39	16	5	23	15	31	65	54
St. Mary, Iflington	14	5	9	6	1	3	1	16	33	
St. Mary, Lambeth	39	11	28	19	2	9	6	10	66	
St. Mary. Mag. Bermondf.	24	8	16	10	7	6	4	70	66	
St. Mary, Whitechapel	19	1	18	12	1	6		8		51
St. Mary, Newington	10		10	3		7	1		14	52
St. Mary, Rotherhithe	20		20	11	4	9	5	36	55	56
St. Matth. Bethnal Green	16		16	16	5			41		
St Paul, Shadwell	21	9	12	9	2	3	3	22		
Parishes in Weftminfter.										
St. Ann, Weftminfter. *	24	9	15	5	1	10	5	20	50	34
St. Clement Dane *	31	6.	25	6	4	19	17	66	90	137
St. Geo. Hanov. Square	142	32	110	47	10	63	44	21	70	34,35
St. James Weftminfter	71	38	33	12	6	21	14	50	66	34
St. John Evang. and St. Mary, Weftminfter	108	20	88	60	17	28	18	28	64	34
St. Martin, in the Fields.	101	37	64	34	12	30	20	35	66	35
St. Mary, Strand	3	1	2	1		1	1	50	100	
St. Paul, Covent-garden*	15	4	11	6	3	5	2	50	40	35

Upon

Upon which I have made the following general Obfervations :

1. That fome few parifhes mention children of former years, dif-charged and delivered in thofe years, which is confounding the defign of the act, and making work to no end.

2. That moft of the parifhes are deficient in mentioning, where children are nurfed ; and though it is to be prefumed, if no mention is made, that it was in the workhoufe, where there is one ; yet it ought to be exprefly declared, that we may fee what the parifhes are about.

3. That the difcharge from the workhoufe, in order to be nurfed, need not be inferted, where it is mentioned *when* and *to whom* they are given to be nurfed; for this alfo is a repetition which only creates unneceffary writing.

4. The taking this general furvey of all the regifters of the parifhes which have any number worth mentioning, is more than I originally intended, being frightened with the bulk of paper : but as in moft other cafes, the nearer we approach objects, the bolder we become, I have ventured fo far. As to minute animadverfions, I have neither time nor inclination to go deeper for the prefent, except it be in one inftance, which ftrikes me with more horror and indignation than any thing I have yet met withal, either in this or any other labori-ous enquiry of the kind.

5. The object in queftion is the conduct of the officers of St. Cle-ment Danes. I had the pleafure (page 51) to make fome acquaintance with good nurfe *Howe,* who upon the face of the regifter, took fuch excellent care of the children belonging to *Whitechapel.* It is true thofe were of 2 and 3 years of age; and thefe I am now about to fpeak of are 3 of 1 and 2 years old, 4 new-born, and the re-mainder of 1 to 7 months old. But furely Mrs. nurfe *Poole* (for

T

that

that is the woman's name) was not caſt in the ſame mold, or com-
poſed of the ſame atoms, as Mrs. *Howe.*

6. Mrs. Poole had, in the year of our Lord MDCCLXV. the
nurſing of XXIII children, belonging to St. Clement Danes, the regiſter of whoſe pariſh is particular in this, that it runs three of the
deaths into January 1766, and this affords ſo much the clearer idea
of the *memorable* tranſaction. The account of the 23 children
ſtands thus:

Diſcharged at the age of 2 years —— —— 1
Ditto of 5 months —— —— —— 1
Remaining alive —— —— —— 3
Departed out of this tranſitory life, in her hands, after
    breathing the vital air, about *one month* —— 18

7. For this *piece of ſervice to the pariſh,* Mrs. Poole has been paid
2 s. each *per* week, which, conſidering the importance of the enter-
prize, muſt be deemed a very *moderate price.*

8. Nurſe *Sadd* had 5 of their children, of whom there is 1 diſcharged, and only 1 dead, and conſequently ſhe is a good woman
as far as I know.

9. Now in the name of the *Father of mercy,* let theſe pariſh officers give Mrs. Poole ſome other employment. She is certainly not
qualifyed for a nurſe, to keep children *alive,* though ſhe ſeems to
underſtand the art of *lulling* infants to their everlaſting reſt. I for-
bear, in this publication, to mention the *names* of the pariſh officers,
though the taſk I have undertaken might juſtify it. *I hope they will
repent and ſin no more.* If this event doth not raiſe indignation,
farewell to all our pretenſions to humanity!

10. In

10. In the F. H. we eſtabliſhed a rule, that if a woman buried 2 children, ſhe ſhould not have a third to nurſe; preſuming that if ſhe was not careleſs, nor wicked, ſhe was unfortunate. In our hurry, *with thouſands*, we deviated from our rule, and the ſame woman might, in a few inſtances, be charged with 3 or 4, one after another: but where is the boundary of St. Clement Danes? This woman began to prepare ſhrowds on the 19th of March 1765, and her laſt burial was on the 25th of Jan. 1766.

11. What the officers may have to ſay in their own defence, it is the precept of liberty and law to hear. They have ſigned the regiſter in all due form, and I conclude, had no intention to impoſe upon the public, much leſs to injure it.

12. But ſo it is: this original deputy of heaven to govern the earth, and to ſubdue it to obedience; this lord and paragon, this miracle of excellency, is himſelf a *ſlave* to *cuſtom*, and ſubject to be metamorphoſed into a *monſter*, even to the devouring of his own ſpecies. The deer, when ſmitten and marked out for deſtruction, is by their inſtinct of ſelf-preſervation abandoned by his kind. The rational animal, from his paſſions and his reaſon, if he is in the order the God of nature intended, flies to the ſuccor of his kind, that is *unjuſtly ſmitten*. This is the *dictate* of humanity; this is the *genius* of liberty; this is the *ſpirit* of laws.

13. The conſideration now before us goes farther ſtill: the great *Deliverer* of man from his *ſlavery* to ſin; the great Judge of the whole earth, ſhewed a regard to children as the objects of his peculiar tenderneſs: if we look on, and ſee ſo *peculiar* a *cruelty* to them, for no other reaſon than becauſe they are *poor*, where will be *our* humanity, *our* liberty, or *our* religion?

14. But

14. But in the fecret workings of that merciful Providence which
" *fhapes our ends, rough hew them how we will*," I am in hopes thefe
St. Clement Danes parifh officers will be the inftruments of the greateft
good to us ; and that which at prefent feems to be fo fmall an object
of humanity, hardly cognizable by any law, may become a ferious
matter of our attention, that we may not depart from the law which
forbids the *deftruction of our fpecies,* whatever the *poors law* may wink
at ; nor from the law of Chrift, whatever the *cuftom* of fome parifhes
may *countenance.*

15. The fallacy of the argument which thefe officers ufe, that
they *cannot do better*, will then appear as *trifling*, as it is *unjuft* and
cruel.   The whole matter is reduced to this : if perfons chofen into
parifh offices are as indolent as men of fortune too often are, and lefs
humane ; if they are not *checked*, they will remain in this evil habit,
becaufe it creates fo much lefs labor and expence to them.   It is
obvious that a little more induftry, fenfe and virtue, and a little
more money are neceffary : and if we cannot find fo much fenfe and
virtue in one part of the town, we muft *remove the object* to another :
and if we cannot raife the money by one means, we muft raife it by
another : but the thing muft be done ; for if we look on with our eyes
open, and are *paffive*, we fhall become partakers in this fanguinary
cruelty and oppreffion.

16. If we go on, we may in time forget that the *life* of man is fur-
rounded, as it were, with flaming fwords, held up by an angel from
heaven : why are thefe poor infants to be left without a *guard*, unlefs it be provided by a real miracle ? In a cafe where thefe officers are
defendant, judge, jury, and *executioner*, and think it *their intereft* that
the *prifoner fhould die*; being fpeechlefs, that he cannot plead, and

2   bound

bound in a *loathfome* dungeon, from whence he is not removed into a fituation of having *a fair trial for his life*, what but a *miracle* can fave him? Where is the genius of our nation, our liberty, or our laws!—God forbid that we fhould longer fee this cafe, or any other, through fo falfe a medium, as to trample upon *that* juftice and humanity, the *conftitution* of which *no cuftom* can alter.

THE END.

For EU product safety concerns, contact us at Calle de José Abascal, 56–1°, 28003 Madrid, Spain or eugpsr@cambridge.org.